BHAKTI BLOSSOMS

2017
GOLDEN DRAGONFLY PRESS

BLOSSOMS

A Collection of
Contemporary Vaishnavi Poetry

Edited by
KRISHNA KANTA DASI

FIRST PRINT EDITION, August 2017
FIRST EBOOK EDITION, August 2017

Copyright © 2017 by Catherine L. Schweig.
Front Cover Design: © Raghu Consbruck, raghudesigns.com

All rights reserved.

First published in the United States of America
by Golden Dragonfly Press, 2017.

No part of this document may be reproduced or transmitted in any form
or by any means, electronic or otherwise, without prior written permission
by the copyright owner.

www.goldendragonflypress.com

We lovingly offer this book to
The Supreme Goddess of Bhakti,
Srimati Radharani—Krishna's dearest beloved—
on the half-moon night
of the lunar month of Bhadra,
on which she made her auspicious appearance.

This book is dedicated to the extraordinary women
of the Bhakti tradition, and unto all those
whose spiritual lives have been enriched by them.

CONTENTS

Foreword   Graham M. Schweig, Ph.D.   xv

Introduction   Krishna Kanta Dasi   xix

Invocation   Vrindavanesvari Aguilera   xxiii

CHAPTER ONE — 1
BHAKTI

The Heart of Bhakti	Pranada Comtois	3
Warning	Dhyana Rico	7
Endless Devotion	Radha Mulder	8
The Way of Bhakti	Madhava Lata Devi Dasi	10
Racing Home	Alexandra Moga	12
Come, My Sweet Love	Gloriana Amador Aguero	13
Sweet, Sweet Honey	Jasmine Kang	14
Our Divine Beloved	Subhadra	15
The Effulgent Moon Dance	Taylor F. Bailey	16
Searching For You	Swati Prabhu K.	17
Seeker	Nirvani Teasley	18
Pluck my Heart	Ananda Shakti	19
Notes of Love	Braja Sorensen	20
Searching	Vrindavanesvari Aguilera	21
You Found Me	Maira J. De La Cruz	23
My Borrowed Best	Debra Sue Lynn	24
Blue Angel	Vesna Vrindavanesvari	25
What Would The Bulbul Say?	Braja Sorensen	26
Divine Visitation	Radha Cornia	27

CHAPTER TWO
DIVINITY — 29

Our Relationships With Divinity	Reflections by Vrinda Sheth	31
Riddled by Time	Radha Mulder	34
Ode to Paramatma	Vrindavanesvari Aguilera	35
Prayer from the Pillar	Madhava Lata Devi Dasi	37
Subduing Kaliya	Mandali Dasi	39
My Cowherd Boy	Anuradha Keshavi Devi Dasi	41
For Your Pleasure	Urmila Devi Dasi	42
O Lord Hari	Seva-mayi Dasi	43
The Army of Cupid is Marching Ahead	Jahnavi Priya Dasi	44
Madhava	Vrindavani Dasi	47
The Bluish Black Boy	Dr. Prachi Desai	48
Resident of My Heart	Priyanka	49
The Chemist	Sudevi Geary	50
Burst Open the Doors of my Heart	Vicitri Dasi	51
The Dance	Radha Cornia	53
Darshan	Jai Radhika Devi Dasi	56
Radha	Braja Sorensen	58
Radha Krishna's Moon	Krishna Vidya Mitchell	59

CHAPTER THREE
GURU & SANGA — 61

Reflections on Guru and Sanga	Dhanya Rico	63
Show Me the Others	Dhanya Rico	66
Vaikuntha Man	Mandali Dasi	67
Temple of Gratitude	Madhava Lata Devi Dasi	68
A Cry in the Night	Rukmini Walker	70
A Labor of Love	Omika Mali	71
A Life with Purpose	Gandarvika Devi Dasi	75

Prayers to the Guru	Vrindavanesvari Aguilera	77
The Importance of the Spiritual Master	Krishna Priya Dasi	78
The shower head is a god I talk to	Pranada Comtois	79
Gurudev	Aradhana Devi Dasi	80
The Transcendental Sadhu	Devarsi Radhika Devi Dasi	82
Harikatha	Sudevi Geary	83
Just for a Moment	Gopi Kumari Devi Dasi	84
Lion Heart	Mallika Dasi Somershein	85
The Opening of My Heart	Tulasi Kunja Devi Dasi	87
My Soul Savior	Akarsini Radhika Devi Dasi	89
Living Still, In Sound	Jahnavi Harrison	90
Connection	Krishna-mayi Dasi	91

CHAPTER FOUR — 93
OUR SELVES & OTHERS

Our Relationships with Our Selves and Others	Urmila Devi Dasi	95
Who Am I?	Tivra-bhakti Devi Dasi	97
My Dear Inner Critic	Gopika-kanta Dasi	98
Far Away from Goloka	Yasomati Devi Dasi	99
When	Janavi Held	100
Inner Quest	Jennieke Janaki	101
Bless Them	Gopalpreet Taya Malakian	102
Surgeon's Tools	Janavi Held	103
Taking Out the Tumors	Gopi Gita Schomaker	104
Song to Self	Dhanya Rico	106
I Have Been Unmade	Janavi Held	107
Healing the Breaks	Ananda Vrindavan Devi	109
Let Them Flow	Atmesvari Dasi	110
Breathe, Baby, Breathe	Jvalamukhi Devi Dasi	111
The Gold in the Summer	Anuradha Sakhi Devi Dasi	112

Pushkar Camel Festival	Rambhoru Devi Dasi	114
The Witness	Radha Sundari Devi Dasi	115
Vaidiki	Mandali Dasi	117
To Mother Indrani	Raga Swan	118
Reunion	Mandie Howard	120
Vaisnava Farewell	Jahnavi Harrison	122

CHAPTER FIVE 123
MAYA'S MAGIC

Krishna's Illusive and Divine Potencies	Visakha Dasi	125
The Search	Vrindavani Dasi	127
Here Today	Janavi Held	129
The Looney Bin of the Universe	Vrnda Devi Dasi	131
By Chance, a Chaunce	Niscala Dasi	132
Spring	Janavi Held	134
Flower Arrows	Pranada Comtois	136
Masquerade	Tivra-bhakti Devi Dasi	137
Repentance and Remorse	Urmila Devi Dasi	138
My Heart—Your Home	Promila Chitkara	139
Nigh High Travel	Pranada Comtois	140
Tanke for Krishna	Promila Chitkara	141
Ode to Mother Earth	Krsnanandini Devi Dasi	142
Stay On	Sri Sundari Dasi	143
Start to Run	Malini Jurelius	144
The Sand Clock	Yasomati Devi Dasi	145
Salvation for Dummies	Samapriya Devi Dasi	146
Demons of the Heart	Pooja Singh	147
Ah, Yes	Vidya Devi Dasi	148

Dappled Winter Sunshine	Shyamasundari Dasi	149
Stop Cleansing the Cage	Visakha Dasi	150
My Only Wish	Hladini Shakti Devi Dasi	151
This Poem Loves	Zoe Williams	152
The Other Dream	Champak Manjari Dasi	154

CHAPTER SIX   155
PRAYERS

A Conversation with God	Janavi Held	157
Thoughts on Prayer	Nanda Carlson	161
Incense	Gopalpreet Taya Malakian	163
Mandir	Braja Sorensen	164
Temple of the Heart	Krsnaa Mary Devi Dasi Fitch	165
Offering My Heart	Kruti Patel	166
Listen	Krsnaa Mary Devi Dasi Fitch	167
May I Still You...	Indu Arora	169
Do Not Wait to Pray	Gopalpreet Taya Malakian	170
Drunk	Jhilmil Breckenridge	171
Devotee Devotee, Krishna's Calling You	Krsnanandini Devi Dasi	172
Prayer to Conquer the Mind	Kaivalya Sundari Devi Dasi	173
Tears	Krishna Rose	174
The One True Goal	Radha Mulder	175
Petals of Grace	Debra Sue Lynn	176
Sigh	Mahalaksmi Devi Dasi	178
I Surrender unto You	Navakishori Devi Dasi	179
Do You Believe Me Yet?	Jagattarini Dasi	180
Sayana Arati	Anuradha Sakhi Devi Dasi	181
My Heart Sings	Ananda Rupa Devi Dasi	182

CHAPTER SEVEN
SEVA
183

Service is my Constant Companion	Braja Sorensen	185
Learning to Love	Vrnda Priya Devi Dasi	187
Soothe the Suffering of Your Heart	Sumati Govinda	188
The Hand Broom's Grip	Pranada Comtois	189
Graffiti	Bhakti Lata Dasi	191
Tearing Out a Bit of My Heart	Mitravinda Devi Dasi	193
The Beating of My Heart	Devesani Radhika Dasi	194
Kitchen Prayer to Lord Nityananda	Madhava Lata Devi Dasi	195
Once Remembered	Madhavi Lata Dasi	196
The Heart's Beat	Gopalpreet Taya Malakian	197
Nights of Kartika	Shyama Bhakti Devi Dasi	198
Heart of a Vaishnavi	Seva-mayi Dasi	199
How Can I be of Service?	Kelly Noyes	200
To the Source	Urmila Devi Dasi	201
Loving Kiss	Jen Walls	202
I am in Love	Mohini Madhavi Devi Dasi	203
Spinning in Love	Malvika Unnithan	204

CHAPTER EIGHT
DIVINE NATURE
205

Divine Nature	Rukmini Walker	207
The Loud Quiet of Snow	Ananda Vrindavan Devi	209
Watching Snow From An Upstairs Window	Rukmini Walker	210
My Winter's Prayer	Nanda Carlson	211
Making Space	Madhavi Glick	212
Planting Seeds	Radha Cornia	214
Universal Form	Sudevi Geary	215

Spring	Gauri Gopika Devi Dasi	217
Letting Go	Jhilmil Breckenridge	218
Krishna's Abundant Gifts	Dhama-rupini Devi Dasi	220
Flower Whispers	Bhakti Lata Dasi	221
To Be a Flower For Krishna	Narayani Devi Dasi	222
Prayers From a Rose	Tulasi D. Estrella	224
Lessons from the Gentle Flower	Jai Gaurangi Devi Dasi	226
Mandarin Infused	Kitzia Kokopelmana	227
Recipients	Laura Smith	228
Monsoon Rains	Anjali Sharma	229
Mayapur Storms	Narayani Devi Dasi	230
Monsoon Krishna	Ananda Vrindavan Devi	231
Monsoon Man	Krsnaa Mary Devi Dasi Fitch	233
Yamuna	Krishna Rose	234
Only Thee	Ananda Shakti	235
Sister of Yamaraja	Daya Dhara Devi Dasi	236
In the Forest of Vrinda	Niscala Dasi	237

CHAPTER NINE 239
THE HOLY NAMES

My Relationship with The Holy Name	Arcana siddhi Devi	241
Spark	Dhanya Rico	243
Mantra Lullaby	Kadamba Mala Devi Dasi	244
Ode to the Holy Name	Jahnavi Harrison	246
On the Beads of Love, I Chant Your Name	Promila Chitkara	247
Mantra's Embrace	Krishna Kanta Dasi	248
Mending My Heart	Ananta Devi Dasi	250
Seduce This Soul	Radha Cornia	251
Holy Name	Braja Sorensen	252

When I Just Sit and Chant	Mohini Madhavi Devi Dasi	253
A Prayer	Vrindvani Dasi	254
Bail	Alexandra Moga	255
Your Name	Jasmine Kang	256
There	Kathamrita Devi Dasi	258
Kirtan Forever!	Mohini Madhavi Devi Dasi	260
A Ratha Yatra Meditation	Yasomati Devi Dasi	261
Captured	Seva-mayi Dasi	262
Lord Krishna's Glorious Holy Name	Krishna Priya Dasi	263
Seeds of Liberation	Meenakshi	264
Dancing God	Paraschiva Florescu	265
Nothing More to Say	Krsnaa Mary Devi Dasi Fitch	266

Note on Style and Spelling of Names	269
About the Authors	271
Glossary	297
Acknowledgements	305

FOREWORD

"Divinity blooms with great joy in places where women are honored; but where women are not honored, all activities are rendered fruitless."
MANU SMRITI 3.56

If you wish to honor the longings of the feminine heart, listen to the words of these poets. If you desire to experience the devotion coming from those whose hearts have been offered to the divine, listen to the words of these poets. I call upon the men and women of this world to hear the yearning, to hear the crying, to hear the singing of women whose hearts have been mostly unheard for centuries and centuries. Let go of any preconceptions or hesitations, and release yourself into these fresh revelations from these poets—contemporary women whose words will engulf your heart as they teach us all how to listen.

Bhakti is a practice that cultivates purity of heart, selflessness of devotion, and sweetness of character. And it is the Vaishnava tradition—centered upon the loving worship of Vishnu, or Krishna, and arising from the Hindu complex of traditions in sacred India—that showcases the practices of Bhakti. This book represents the first time in the history of this millennia-old Vaishnava tradition that a collection of poems by Vaishnavis (female practitioners within the Vaishnava tradition) is presented.

Even though Vaishnava lineages in several cases contain links filled by great Bhakti yoginis, the female voice of Bhakti has not received the kind of attention it has deserved throughout the centuries. Over decades of studying and researching the Krishna Bhakti traditions, I have observed a kind of backseat given to the voices of women. Even though the main Bhakti text of the *Bhagavata Purana* brings out the voices of great Vaishnavis, such as Kunti, Devahuti, and the Vraja Gopikas—who are extolled as the supreme devotees of Krishna in his divine play of the Rasa Dance—women's voices have remained, for the most part, in the background.

In the past century, however, women's practices of Bhakti are very gradually being valued as much of those of their male counterparts. This shift in attitude toward receiving and respecting the participation of women is more on the social level than it is in the scriptural writings of the tradition, for these ancient texts can, at times, appear to depict women as inferior to their male counterparts. But when the tradition is examined carefully, we find that female perception and intelligence is not only *not inferior* to that of men, but indeed, the feminine view is intrinsically invaluable for gaining a total perspective of the gifts the Vaishnava tradition has to offer the world.

This book allows us to hear the neglected feminine voice in Bhakti and to begin appreciating how the female perspective is informed by a special kind of intelligence, or *medha*, as stated in the *Bhagavad Gita* (Chapter 10, verse 34). *Medha* is as critical to understanding aspects of the Divine as *buddhi*, or the masculine intelligence, is. *Medha* and *buddhi* must work together, as all genders must cooperate in harmony with one another, to obtain a complete picture of our relationship to the Divine. This volume is a unique contribution toward that more informed vision of Divinity, and to the history of Vaishnava literature and expression, as it exclusively honors those voices that flow with *medha*.

Join me now as we enter into an uplifting realm: a realm filled with the many feelings and emotions surrounding spiritual journeys. It is the realm of the rich spiritual intelligence bestowed to women steeped in devotional love for God, or the divine: rare souls immersed in the practice of Bhakti, or "the offering of one's whole heart to divinity." May we receive them as they bring more Bhakti into a world that so desperately needs their voices. May they teach us all to listen to the Bhakti all around us, and within us, regardless of gender! And may our hearts find spiritual nourishment in the pages that follow.

>   Graham M. Schweig, Ph.D.
>   Professor of Philosophy & Religion
>   Christopher Newport University, Virginia
>   Distinguished Teaching & Research Fellow
>   Graduate Theological Union, Berkeley
>   Author-translator of *Bhagavad Gita:*
>   *The Beloved Lord's Secret Love Song*

INTRODUCTION

*"Hoping to blossom (one day) into a flower,
Every bud sits, holding its soul in its fist."*
MAHLAQA BAI CHANDA (1767-1824)

We all possess the capacity to enchant God, or Krishna, with a heart that has fully blossomed in Bhakti, or devotional love. The ancient Bhakti traditions overflow with poetic flower metaphors that depict the relationships souls have to the Divine: the tighter the bud the more resistant we are to Bhakti, the more our petals open, the more awake our heart is to receiving and reciprocating the love God has for us.

At the heart of the ancient Bhakti texts, in the tenth book of the *Bhagavata Purana*, we encounter a beautiful flower blossom made up of a community of women known as the Gopis. These 108 cowherd women unite in a circular dance—called the *rasa mandala*—that mirrors the many petals of a fully blossomed lotus flower. Under autumn's reddish moon, in the jasmine-scented forest of Vraja, the Gopis link arms as they dance around the supreme vision of divine love in the Bhakti sacred texts: Radha, the Divine Feminine, and Krishna, the Divine Masculine.

This linking of arms between the Gopis represents the power of community, or sanga, celebrated in Bhakti culture. It is through inspiring one another and sharing our spiritual journeys that our tight little buds begin to unfurl. The night of the rasa dance, the Gopis together composed the most exalted verses in the Bhakti literature, revealing a love so selfless and pure that God himself felt incapable of reciprocating it!

Descending from the line of the Gopis, the poetic voices of women in this book represent a devoted community of contemporary Bhakti yoginis from all over the world uniting to offer us a rare glimpse into their devotional hearts. Although some are new to writing poetry—and one-third of the participants engage English as their second language—the 108 authors nevertheless paint an honest and inspiring portrait of what it's like to be a woman practicing Bhakti today, including the perspectives of those who have just begun a Bhakti practice, seasoned practitioners of several decades, and those who were born into the Bhakti path.

This rare collection of poems is divided into nine rich themes all revolving around the power of relationships in Bhakti. The book begins with two chapters full of love poems to Krishna, and colorful descriptions of his beauty, compassion, mercy and might. Introduced by Pranada Comtois and Vrinda Sheth, these first poems often appear to echo the separation and longing sentiments of the Gopis, as the poets recount divine *lilas* (sacred pastimes from the tradition) and their own relationships to them.

Chapters three and four, introduced by Dhanya Rico and Urmila Dasi, revolve around the Vaishnavis' relationships with themselves and others, including their bodies, their families, the *sangas*—or communities they live in—as well as the special relationships they have with their individual gurus. The importance of cultivating an atmosphere of trust, in which real sharing can occur, is emphasized. In Rico's words: "Whether we are joining together to chant the Maha-Mantra or share spiritually inspiring poetry, it requires a great deal of vulnerability to sit and truly open your heart in this way."

The fifth chapter presents brave and honest accounts of struggles in the spiritual practices of the poetesses. From existential angst to frustration with the material world, the *maya* chapter holds expressions of repentance and remorse, feeling abandoned and fighting demons within. Complete with an insightful introduction by Vishaka Dasi, it also paints philosophical pictures of the temporary nature of the material realm, time, and the concept of a real home. In her words: "the poets remark on both aspects of *maya*—the delusive one that causes us to suffer the effects of time, as well as the divine one that draws us to Krishna's transcendent world."

From struggles, the book introduces us to *vandanam*, or prayers: after a beautiful introduction by Janavi Held, the poets then take us into their personal dialogues with God. We hear of different kinds of praying, from achy surrendering to feeling comforted by divine grace. Like with Queen Kunti—an exalted Bhakti yogini of antiquity—calamities seem to deepen the poets' connection to Krishna, and adversity is engaged as fuel in their *sadhana*, or spiritual practice. The women's prayers are gentle and fierce at once, flowing out in tears, sighs, pleas, and songs.

Chapter seven is all about *sevanam*, or service, and begins with an introduction by Braja Sorensen in which *seva* is equated with *sanatana-dharma*: our eternal religion, or occupation. Here, the broad vision of the Vaishnavi poets relates to a variety of activities as *seva*: everything from sweeping the floor, cooking and playing *mridanga* (drum), to chanting on the streets, mending heart-wounds and learning to be closer to others, all become activities that can be engaged in the practice of Bhakti yoga.

The book's enticing penultimate chapter overflows with beautiful descriptions of the way the poets' individual relationships with Nature inspire their love for God. Introduced by Rukmini Walker, the eighth chapter illuminates moments of peaceful introspection as snow descends or birds sing, or a monsoon cloud arouses thoughts of Krishna's complexion. Here, the Vaishnavis' appreciation for the power and beauty of Mother Nature reveals the power and beauty of the Supreme Divinity, Krishna. These sweet conversations with seasons, flowers, rainstorms, and sacred rivers offer us a way of seeing Divinity everywhere.

The final poems that appear in the book are all dedicated to the authors' dynamic relationships to the mantra that is central to the Chaitanya Bhakti tradition, or the *maha* mantra. After a very sweet and personal chapter introduction by Arcana Siddhi Devi Dasi, the verses soar with poetic narratives about chanting the

Holy Names: listening to them, feeling embraced by them, saved by them, healed by them. The words of the Vaishnavi poets lead us into congregational *kirtans* as well as private *japa*, or chanting, sessions, as they illuminate the soothing, transformative, and liberating power of mantra meditation.

This collection of poems by contemporary Vaishnavis acts as a testament to the spiritual wisdom, strength, and beauty contained in the precious voices of our mothers, grandmothers, sisters, daughters, nieces, and wives in the Bhakti tradition. Imbibing the spirit of the poetic Gopis, and of Radha—their poet queen, or *Kavirani*—the women in this book make an important contribution toward the resurgence of the feminine voice in the modern Bhakti sangas. Their poems presented as individual Bhakti-blossoms, strung together in a garland of love, offered unto all those whose hearts are ripe.

INVOCATION

We offer our respects to the goddess of verse:
With reverence, dear Sarasvati
Humbly
Submissively
Simply
For it is you who regulates
the flow, the come and go,
the opening and closing of the gates.
You; guardian of fate,
of poetry!
We entreat you, dear goddess:
Approaching with folded palms
we rest our fears and qualms
at your feet,
oh servant of Radha,
that ultimate Kavirani;
Poetess Supreme!

VRINDAVANESVARI AGUILERA

CHAPTER ONE

BHAKTI

"Truly, Bhakti is that which
is offered unto the Beloved
by one who is wholly devoted
with purest love, Prema—
this is its very form."

The Bhakti Sutra of Narada, Text 2
Translation by Graham M. Schweig

The Heart of Bhakti

Pranada Comtois

Central to the ancient Bhakti traditions is Radha, the feminine energy of the Divine, who reveals the desirable prospect of cultivating a relationship with our Source, Krishna. Such a sacred liaison naturally makes all other relationships pale in comparison.

Radha escorts us beyond mundane relationships—which so often fail us—into the eternal home of the heart. There, our souls lovingly play with Krishna in a divine relationship of ever-fresh exchanges. Such boundless expressions of pure love have been immortalized in the most prominent of sacred Bhakti texts: the ancient *Bhagavata Purana*. Of all these expressions, Radha's love for Krishna is at the center, and it is she who invites us to inhabit our eternal hearts and enter into our own loving relationship with the perfect object of love.

I was formally initiated into the Bhakti path at age seventeen, decades ago when it first took root in America. Over the years, I have learned that life presents us with two main paths: the liberating and heartfelt path of Bhakti, or the binding, body-oriented path of karma. Karma stringently rules our physical existence, while Bhakti gently governs our soul. Karma spurs *taking*, while Bhakti promotes *giving*. Enmeshed in karma we suffer miseries of the mind and body. Immersed in Bhakti we experience the joy of the self. It is our choice which path we take. Appropriately, choosing wisely is tantamount to our ability to thrive and be joyful in life.

I have found that the secret of living a happy life hinges on this simple premise: we can choose to give instead of take. Our needs are met beyond our expectations when we give to our Source, who, as the reservoir of love, is capable of fully reciprocating in ways no one else can. When we take this approach, we find that our consciousness expands beyond the bounds of instinct and human reason into exalted love. Through giving in Bhakti we receive real treasures of the self as we're ushered into the timeless world of spiritual love: the beautiful world where Radha reigns.

More than philosophy or specific spiritual practices, Bhakti, also known as Radha is the full form of love; she is the external manifestation of the Absolute's heart. Radha's singular desire is to please her beloved, Krishna, and her mastery at doing so is acknowledged by Krishna himself, who says that Radha is *his* guru in the dance of love. As such, Radha is also the guru for all those on the Bhakti path. Yes, the Bhakti traditions start with a female guru and adore—along with God—the feminine divine!

Radha's supreme example demonstrates the most magical aspect of Bhakti: how giving becomes receiving when we offer our love to the perfect object of love, our Supreme Source. Radha is the emblem of a perfect giver. No matter how much she gives, she is never depleted but remains always blossoming brilliantly in the highest ecstasy, ever displaying the perfection of giving to the fully capable object of love. By engaging one's heart, mind, body, and words in the service of Krishna, we will never be drained, reduced, or depreciated. He is ever grateful, generous, sweet, and responds with utmost attention to each of us individual souls according to how we love him. Radha entreats us to experience this for ourselves.

Through my own Bhakti practices, I've gradually entered into a captivating relationship with Radha. As her influence expands in me, I've found she responds to the intensity of my desire, and my service, in kind. In other words, I experience Bhakti as a dynamic exchange between hearts—my own and Radha's—in which, every aspect of my life is personally tailored to the way I relate to her. Through Radha's grace, Bhakti's powers regularly transport me into my heart's innermost territory and inspire me how to walk in this difficult world with gratitude and grace.

As a woman today, I feel that I am in an especially privileged position to naturally practice bhakti. Despite any discouragement I've endured on the outside (and there has been much!), on the inside my heart remains eager to love my Divine Significant Other, Krishna. Through hearing, singing, and speaking in loving praise of Krishna I've been given unexpected glimpses into my true self, which is beyond the world-imposed limitations of the body. In cultivating this vision, I have surprisingly learned to appreciate my soft feminine qualities, and the ways they feed my Bhakti heart.

The feminine energy of the Divine, Radha, being very gentle and compassionate, is always inclined to extend us mercy. Yet, because many in this world dishonor her Beloved, relationships between humans, the world, and the Supreme have become disharmonious. The feminine divine that flows through us in Bhakti is the great Heroine that will mend these relationships and return them to their natural, loving state. It is my conviction that Bhakti is the doorway to solving our problems, and that women hold the keys to that doorway.

This is because we women are blessed as instinctive givers. We can draw upon our natural feminine qualities early in the practice of Bhakti to understand—and enter more deeply into—the nature of spiritual love and service. It is unfortunate if the voices of women in the Bhakti tradition are pushed into the background when selfish masculine traits dominate, like the desire for power, profit, and prestige. I have personally faced such barriers and witnessed the way they cause Bhakti to withhold her innermost secrets.

The devoted and diverse women in this volume of poems, however, brave all obstacles to share some of Bhakti's most precious secrets with us. Offering a wonderful window into Bhakti's sweet nature, these women have begun to grasp Radha's unstoppable power: the power pure love has to capture the heart of God! In these poems, we hear women forming a loving alliance with Radha as they imbibe her compassion and guidance.

I believe that by serving Radha *all* women hold the power to change the world. By taking to the generous way of the feminine divine—bolstered by their natural giving tendencies—women are well suited to model a very different way of life than the one that takes away from others and from our abused planet. We will then all be in for a spiritual renaissance the likes of which have never been seen before! Radha is personally inviting us to be the agents of change to provoke this spiritual revolution.

In *Bhakti Blossoms* we hear the stirring of this revolution begin, as we are gently ushered into the private, inner gardens of women who are bound in a loving exchange with the fountainhead of all goddesses, Sri Radha. Following Radha, these women are on an ardent, pressing search for their lover, Krishna. Let us now tread delicately as we enter into the first chapter of this garden of bhakti blossoms; that some of their pollen may make our own hearts more fertile.

Warning

Dhyana Rico

The fear. The fear.
The scent of it lingers in the plains.

Love, like a wild wind
Gathers and grows
If I close my eyes and say
"Brave"
I can hear it
Howling to me.
"I have come for you,
Consider this fair warning."

Endless Devotion
Radha Mulder

Drizzly rain had come again,
but they danced on just the same,
The Earth shook with every step,
ankle bells chimed and their eyes met.

Suddenly She stopped, overcome,
her beautiful hair falling undone.

Her heart swelled with overwhelming emotion,
swimming in pools of endless devotion.

"What is it my dear?" He asked again,
she tried to answer, *alas* in vain,

For Her heart raced,
Her breathing in haste,

Her cheeks brightly flushed,
when Her words suddenly rushed:

"With each step, each move, each glance of Yours,
my heart surrenders, it yearns and implores.

With each step, the waves of love increase,
my heart feeling as if it may cease.

For Love is an ocean in which I continuously drown,
and You are the harbor where I am safely found."

He responded to Her heart's desire,
and spoke these words to quench the fire:

"Oh my dear, my love, my life unending,
my heart feels as if it's eternally ascending!

It goes on and on and flows thru forever,
becoming stronger and braver, no matter the weather!

For Love is this rain that gently pours,
and You are the shelter my heart seeks for!"

The Way of Bhakti

Madhava Lata Devi Dasi

Evam... in this way
the night again falls after day,
the milky stars fall beyond the horizon
on their revolving way,
and ghee falls into the fire,
and the Source-of-All
with the souls re-unite,
thus, the Universe speaks:
motion is a wheel
as you receive
offer back
do not keep
as the tree only gives
for some water that it receives,
but does not hold nor taste
how its fruit is sweet.

Do not take, neither keep—
always give back
and put love in your hands
without holding back,
'cause it was given like that.
whatever we have is a gift,
do not grab anything
lest envy, lust and greed
hold your heart
in a dark grip;

from the air we receive our life
from the earth the plants

to stay alive
and emotions from a beautiful sky
from the stars a cuddle to sleep
even darkness gives us dreams
and we rejoice at the flowers,
the sun rays, the cool breezes
but do not forget, it is not ours
it is received,
gratefully reciprocate,
love means to always give,
in this way
with Bhakti
turn the universal wheel.

Racing Home
Alexandra Moga

do you think the lover
on the way to her Beloved
can see anything but
love?
be like that lover
all racing,
unapologetic
and so resolutely
focused
that this life is just one
blurry
ride
home

Come, My Sweet Love

Gloriana Amador Aguero

Krishna calls us:
Come, my sweet love, come.
Because you belong to your Beloved,
and your Beloved belongs to you.
Come my darling, come.

You have searched for so long
without finding me.
I have captivated your heart.
I called you and dried your tears.

Come, my sweet love, come.
Leave your house and your people,
your heart bows to me.
Come my darling, come…

I'll let you see my gardens and flowers,
I'll let you dance in front of me,
I'll hear you singing,
I'll hear you laughing.

Come, my sweet love, come.
From your heart flows the sweetest honey.
I have touched your soul with my love.
Come my darling, come…

(Inspired by The Song of Solomon)

Sweet, Sweet Honey

Jasmine Kang

Sweet, sweet honey,
golden ray of light!
Here I come, here I go,
like the waves of the ocean,
like the wind that blows.

I hear the song of a flute
with a sweet melody!
Carried by the wind
like rain falling on my heart;
I dance to its tune.

Sing, sweet melody…
You call out to my heart!
Like a songbird sings a love song,
like a rose draws honeybees:
I am Yours! You are mine!

Sweet, sweet honey
Dripping from a rose!
I hear my heart say:
"You will always be near me
as I will be near You."

Our Divine Beloved
Subhadra

Oh love!
How much I long to express your enchanting names!
To feel the scent of your presence,
and the gaze of your soft eyes
which watch me from your abode,
kissed by the sweetness
of your eternal presence
closer to me than my breath itself.

This inner search starts with
your whisper in my heart;
like following a trail of rose petals
leading me deeper into the garden of love.

The more I discover myself
in the light of your love
and in the sacred moments of life
the more I bathe in an outburst of expression:
dancing from the core of my heart
realizing what is already here
in this sacred walk of life…

The Effulgent Moon Dance

Taylor F. Bailey

I am now losing my composure and etiquette.
Let me inquire a few things of you.
Oh, Krishna, there is no reason you should tell me.
Except that I am faithful in addressing only you.
Let us go back to that place
where we sang together while the moon rose.
Let me go through those doors,
as they are now closing,
and my memory is fading.
Let us run wild and dance like it is just us
in the moon's effulgence.
I am now sure of my desire:
Oh, by allowing me to know you,
I can engage in something deeper.
But you must let me in before time runs out.

Searching For You

Swati Prabhu K.

I looked back
because I thought I saw You.

I listened cautiously
because I thought I heard You.

I checked for You when chanting, again and again
because I heard You are Your Holy Names.

When I was in Your devotees' company
I felt Your presence in Your fragrance.

I kept on speaking to You
Because I thought You were around me…
yet found no one around me
only to realize: I'm missing You!

Seeker

Nirvani Teasley

I seek night and day, for just a glimpse of that bliss;
To refresh my depleted soul, to end its weariness with that bliss.

I call near and far, with only echoes for my friends.
My spirit mellows, fatigued of unconsciousness of that bliss.

I shed tears, hollowed out spheres wanting to be filled
with what?
It evades me, time and again, the insatiable kiss of that bliss.

I touched its flighty wings once and screamed ecstatic silence.
I fell delirious into its open arms and still I was dismissed
      by that bliss.

To have tasted of the rapture, but never keep is Nirvani's madness.
And in death, with only a whisper on lips of the awareness
      of that bliss.

Pluck my Heart

Ananda Shakti

My body aches in pain being separated from you
My mind can no longer concentrate
My heart is clenched with longing
My limbs pull away from everyone else
Please release me from this prison!
If you are going to make me love you
bring us together.
Or take my life so that I may find you in that form
sweet Lord Shyam
How much more suffering do you need to see
for me to prove my love?
Just pluck my heart and choose me for your garden.

Notes of Love
Braja Sorensen

each note i play is
a beat of my heart
that sings the song
of my love

fat monsoon raindrops,
footsteps on the earth,
dance to the rhythm
of my love

words laced with ardor
decorate the sky
a lilting chorus
of my love

does He hear me?

Searching

Vrindavanesvari Aguilera

Where are You?

I search for You
I look for You,
I hasten and hurry
Peering in every cranny and nook for You.

I scan the crowds for Your face
I scour every town,
City and space

Where are You?

Are You in the taste of the food I cook?
Are You hidden in the words of a book?
Are You in the falling droplets of rain?
Are You in the silence of a pause,
Or the pierce of sharp pain?
Are You dancing in the melody of a song?
Must I, must I search my whole life long?

Where are You?

Finally, gazing deep within my soul,
I see!
I glimpse Your presence
You've been here all along!

In the woven rhythms of poetry
In the strength of the strong

In the beauty in nature
In the grandeur of a life lived long
In the softness of grace
In the comforting arms of a mother
The sweetness of a lover's embrace

I see You!
You're all over the place!

You've been here, here all along
Waiting for me to turn inwards, upwards
To feel Your love and lilting flute song
So many years I've spent searching
Much time wasted in a futile chase
When I'd only to turn inwards to feel the warmth of Your embrace

The path is in the search
The journey and destination share the same trails
Heart's fulfillment in Bhakti
The wind that fills my soul's sails

May I search for eternity
Finding you again and again

You Found Me

Maira J. De La Cruz

I am found!
No longer lost in the concrete jungle of the world.
I see the fresh path that is true and green.

Thus, I sing to you with cymbals of gratitude
and drums that beat your love and glories
into the hearts of the sincere.

Love.
Like a giant wave that crashes…
Plundering and purifying…
Inundating the city of nine gates
where the soul lies asleep.

Wake up sleeping souls!
Stop dreaming up illusions!

No time to waste.
Time is life. Time is death.

The divine sun that is your soul within
wishes to rise above the dark clouds of ignorance.

Blazing light.
Smiling rays.
I see truth.

My Borrowed Best

Debra Sue Lynn

Silence comes to find me
lost in quintessential song of love;
And tacitly reminds me, one cannot possess
the butterfly, nor the dove.
So fly my beloved, my borrowed best.
Then come ye home and find ye rest
succored at the Lord's supple breast.

Blue Angel

Vesna Vrindavanesvari

Walking into Your eyes
with every step
further away You have seemed
as I melted inside.
Colored for good in a daunting sway.
Who were You?
And why, on Earth have you captured my mind?
Is it real?
Is Life meant for us to seek and find?
For I lost myself in finding You!
I saw an Angel today
and he pierced my heart
to stop me from running away from Love.
Turning to me
He touched me, to stop me
from running away from Love.
Glance of union:
breaking the doors, crushing the walls down
to a heavenly Lover.
He pierced my Heart
to stop me from running away,
to drown me in the call of His eyes,
to guide the way to eternal Loving.
That day, like glass, my reality shattered
in the ray of His Light:
A new vision for my sight
as I float into the unseen
with calmness and power
as I navigate, I'm born anew:
Liberated into His love.

What Would the Bulbul Say?

Braja Sorensen

what would the bulbul say
were he to hear the longing
of my silent heart?

the notes he sings are leaves
who fall like teardrops from trees
unable to bear the pain

would the sun flee, too shy to watch
and let darkness, deep like your voice,
sweep in

his song, sweet and light,
whispers breath into the flute
whose notes rejoice in the embers of day

its sweet song melts the lock of hope
that keeps my life-breath in the
burning house of my body

i bathe in the golden waters of thoughts
whose cooling splash becomes
the altar for my mind

Divine Visitation

Radha Cornia

My dreaming eyes beheld a room swept bare
Of all the clutter from my waking hours
White walls and wooden floors encountered there
And the fragrance of night blooming jasmine flowers
Sunlight broke through on the windowsill
Then danced upon the walls like golden lace
I saw the sunlight and my heart grew still
Enraptured by the quiet of that place
All at once I felt a presence there
I heard a footstep brush across the floor
Like peacock feathers soft upon the stair
Then sweet Madhana entered at my door
Illuminated like the sky at dawn
When all the world is rendered fresh and clear
My heart grew lighter as I gazed upon
The beauty of His face as He drew near
Clothed in honey silk and tawny pearls
Garland made of Tulasi and of rose
Pink as the blushing cheeks of maiden girls
Who could not be lovelier in His clothes
Black hair caressed His cheeks and caught the light
Reflected from His luminescent face
I felt my body tremble at the sight
I prayed I might surrender to His grace
Then fell before Him on the wooden floor
Tempted by the shelter of His feet
The fragrance of the flowers that he wore
Was intoxicating, mystically sweet.
He smiled and my head began to reel
Inebriated by one sacred glance

That loosed my grip on Maya Devi's wheel
As I yielded to celestial romance
But tears were in my eyes when I awoke
Grieving for a treasure that is lost
I cannot recall the words He spoke
And in my waking world I pay the cost
Let me gratefully forgo the morning sun
Eternally renounce my waking role
Content if I can only gaze upon
That ethereal seducer of my soul

CHAPTER TWO

DIVINITY

"Upon hearing the flute of Govinda,
peacocks dance in rapture—
Observing their dancing from hilltops,
all other creatures
become stunned."

Spoken by the Vraja Gopikas,
VENU GITA TEXT 10

Our Relationships with Divinity
Reflections by Vrinda Sheth

There is so much in this world that divides us human beings from one another. Our identities are comprised of many subtle layers, starting with gender, race, nationality, and spiraling outward into concerns of sexuality, social status, and religious beliefs. We are constantly evolving in our understanding of what is crucial to our development, and most of us have complex relationships with all the various aspects of ourselves. We do, however, have one obvious and common denominator: although we may die alone, not one among us is ever born alone.

By nature's design, we all have a mother, every one of us. In this fact, we stand united. Through the union of our father and mother we were created: a new, unique being. We are therefore creatures of relationship. You and I began our lives relating to our mother, and hopefully, a father too. But what was it that propelled us into these bodies we inhabit? Is there a mastermind behind it all? Is there a divine relationship that has the power to eclipse our earthly ones? With such questions, we enter into the realm of the mystics, where divinity—in all its grandeur—starts coming into focus.

For me, a meaningful reflection on divinity begins with a look at my heritage. I take this larger-than-life concept of divinity and bring it home by asking: Who is my parent's God? What does my mother believe? What does my father believe? What did they, together and individually, transmit to me? Where do I stand, as an adult, in relation to what I was taught as a child? Each of us is going to have very unique answers to these reflections—and appropriately so—because the Bhakti yoga tradition teaches that each of us has a personal, individual, and eternal relationship with the Divine.

I am a unique individual and my relationship to divinity is my own: something that no one can ever take from me. I have access to the divine through my heart, especially when the channel is clear and my prayer strong. I don't have to go anywhere but within. My discovery of, and quest for, this eternal heart-connection is ongoing. It continues to circle back to an awareness of what was transmitted to me by my family and my community.

Though I was born in Sweden, one of the most progressive modern countries, I was raised in a small insular village dedicated to becoming Krishna-conscious. One of my earliest childhood memories is of my mother's voice. It would drift into my dreams and wake me up as she walked about our room, softly chanting the Hare Krishna mantra to herself. I found her voice soothing and her demeanor content. By her simple example, she transmitted devotion towards Krishna: the blue-hued cowherd boy, depicted often with a peacock feather in his hair and a flute in his hand. My mother spent practically all her free time creating watercolor paintings of Radha and Krishna, the divine couple: another unique concept of the Bhakti tradition, where the divine is conceived as male and female, two parts of a complete whole.

My father was also a strong presence in my childhood. From him, I learnt that nothing mattered as unequivocally as the quest for self-realization and the release from material bondage. This dedicated focus left little room for family affection and care. In fact, he made such obliterating impressions on me that I was in my late twenties when I began the work of separating my concepts from his. Stronger in my own identity, I now receive with an open heart my father's legacy, while also being able to discern where I stand.

Sometimes, I'm so heartbreakingly grateful for the rich wisdom imparted to me; it feels second nature, like holding the hand of a trusted friend. At other times, I feel suspicious, even angry and cheated, the scars throbbing with fierce will, refusing to be silenced. This opposition, I think, is at the heart of every life. As writer Flannery O'Connor said, "Anybody who has survived his childhood will have enough information about life to last him the rest of his days."

I would like to call the reader's attention to the timely manifestation of *Bhakti Blossoms,* which celebrates the feminine voice, with its unique intelligence. We know that across the board, the female voice has over countless centuries been underrepresented, even willfully excluded. This undeniable drought is causing an equally undeniable thirst for a strong female presence. Women are stepping forward like never before in the fields of art, literature, and film all over the world. I see this collection of poems as another step in that direction: a tribute to the fundamental and necessary shift in our collective consciousness. At the end of the day, gender is a minor concern, for when we shed the mortal frame, the soul remains, and the soul has no limitations. In our pursuit of happiness, this limitless state is what we aspire for even now, every day.

In "Our Relationships to Divinity," the god of my childhood—Krishna—will be referred to by names such as Hari, Madan-Mohan, and Nandulal. The Divine's presence as experienced within our heart is referenced as Paramatma, often translated literally as Supersoul. Even when not overtly mentioned, the poets here transmit a sense of engaging with this Supreme Being who is a loving witness to our lives. As you gain entrance into the hearts of these Vaishnavis, my conviction is that your own relationship with the divine will come alive. In this relationship, you may discover many surprising eruptions, a wealth of feelings that perhaps only poetry can truly express.

Riddled by Time
Radha Mulder

Vast, endless ages I've wandered,
in search of You.

Calling your Name,
thinking perhaps I was going insane.

Across distant galaxies,
swept thru elements and riddled by time,

restless and wondering
when you'd be mine.

But now I realize,
and now I see,

All the while,
You were calling for me.

Ode to Paramatma

Vrindavanesvari Aguilera

How you wait so patiently
Your arms ever open wide
Until your lost children return;
Hearts cleansed of false ego,
False pleasures, false pride

Residing within
Through thick and thin
Innumerable material transmigrations
Witnessing our reactive fortunes and sins

Oh most wonderful being
Seated within our hearts!
How to remember and love you
Is in this world a lost art

You are our ever well-wisher
Our dear most friend
From the inestimable beginning
To the undying end

If only one will turn to you
Like a child to its mother,
Then we will receive guidance
Like no other

All of our insufficiencies
Our insurmountable battles and pain,
Will be soothed away and vanquished
By your holy name

My dear Paramatma
Thank you so much
For traveling with us
Ever loving, ever guiding us
with your gentle touch.

Prayer from the Pillar

Madhava Lata Devi Dasi

My Lion Lord,
I am here,
in this dark dream,
lost and overwhelmed
in the cloudy corner of Your realm,
down,
beyond the Viraja river
on an expanse of water,
in a cluster of bubbles
exhaled from Your breath,
more down,
behind the seven coverings
caused by the false ego,
way down,
within a drop of many drops,
dripped from Your pores
so down,
on one of the billion spheres
floating in space,
down here,
entrapped in fears,
in a form of bleak desires
reduced to a dimmed sparkle
caught between the mind's pliers,
an infinitesimal dot of existence,
where my soul cries
inaudible,
like words shouted in water.
I am here,
a fossil in a pillar

of million of lifetimes
please break it with your claws
take me up
on your lap
from where
fearless I can look—down
at the remains
of this stony heart.

Subduing Kaliya

Mandali Dasi

Venomous snakes
joyously nest
on the crust of my little heart,
dancing and dancing and wildly romancing,
tearing attention apart.

Clusters of jeweled wants and desires,
oh, who is, who is to blame?
Dancing away on a solid terrain,
their folly knows no shame.

Ruby tongues
and envious eyes
search for an easy prey
while they intertwine
to a melody divine
and dance, dance away.

Fastened the belt
and trees start to melt,
it's time for some serious dancing!
A joyous lover
whose step knows no danger,
the snakes have indeed started trembling!
Looks like the jeweled wants and desires
are solid enough to perform.
He mounts on their heads,
and envy He treads,
mastery in absolute form.

Bimba lips rest on the flute,
calling for intimate friends.
An image of truth,
a beautiful youth,
a pastime that never ends.

My Cowherd Boy

Anuradha Keshavi Devi Dasi

Tears trickle across my cheek
as a divine voice sings into my ears
emotions well up in my heart...
If just a mortal voice is so heart-rendering
what must your transcendental voice be like
O bluish-tinged cowherd boy?

For Your Pleasure

Urmila Devi Dasi

The world is full of Your singing
Oh dancing flute player bright!
Sweet is the thrill of your laughing
filling your loves with delight.
Soft is the touch of your ruby-like palms,
full of great joy are your songs,
visions of yours are such soothing balms
for you my heart, for you, ever longs.
How can I please You my love, my Lord?
How make Your pleasure increase?
Cut my illusion with knowledge's sword,
from Maya please grant my release;
Not for the purpose of freedom from pain,
nor for deep spiritual bliss
making your pastimes joyfulness gain,
but for pure motive and heart is my wish.

O Lord Hari

Seva-mayi Dasi

O Lord Hari,
Like an elixir poured out over creation
your energies permeate this mundane world:
infusing it with unfathomable wonders.
What to speak of Your spiritual abode!
Where this symphony of birds before me, who
pirouette with the lulling vibrations of crashing waves,
are less attractive than cawing crows compared
to just one note from Your flute.
Where everything Your lips touch is
gilded with the golden radiance of Your Divine Love.

The Army of Cupid is Marching Ahead

Jahnvi Priya Dasi

Wearing a peacock feather on His head,
sweet *karnikara* flowers adorning His ears,
His yellow silk garment shining like gold,
beautiful *vaijayanti* up to His toes,
the greatest of dancers is ready to begin:
The army of Cupid is marching ahead.

Surrounded by Gopas and maddened bees,
when flying birds see Him they freeze.
With thousands of stars over the of village Vraja,
the moon-like son of Nanda Maharaja
enters the forest with his cowherd friends:
The army of Cupid is marching ahead.

His face is framed by curling locks of hair,
his two imposing arms take away fear,
he moves with the grace of a regal elephant,
while his flute steals the Gopi's ears,
with teeth like new jasmine buds:
The army of cupid is marching ahead.

Adorned in anklets, rings and earrings,
smiling are His beautiful, pinkish lips.
Bow-like brows and arrow-like eyes,
he can shoot straight into our hearts
with His beauty defeating that of the rose bud.
The army of cupid is marching ahead.

Festival for the eyes and heart of hearts,
decorated with love-weapons from toe to top.
His smile can ignite fire in the heart,
His sidelong glance will give you a start.
Reddish eye rims and thick, wavy hair,
His blue complexion is beyond compare!
The army of Cupid is marching ahead.

Tending the cows playing His flute,
He spreads happiness, walking in Govardhan grooves.
He counts His cows on strings of gems,
and gives them pleasure by calling their names.
Difficult to run with full milk bags,
they are also devotees in a different dress:
Shyama, Tilakini, Dhavali and Surabhi,
And look! Here comes arrogant Mridangmukhi!
A herd of cows in love with Govinda.
The army of Cupid is marching ahead.

Upon seeing Him the moving become still,
And the still began to dance,
He is mercifully pulling each jiva,
into an amorous trance.
His words intensify loving devotion,
His beauty causes quite a commotion.
He is the dear most friend of all.
Once who sees Him can't ever fall.
The army of cupid is marching ahead.

Oh dear devotee
do not surrender unto Him.
Fight, fight for His pleasure and fun!
He may not reciprocate with your loving mood,

He wants to nourish your devotional root
He is expert and very keen,
fulfilling you even by impossible means.
Such a Lord has never been seen!
One who loves to be defeated by the love of his devotees.
So fight with Him in this game so sweet
tie up his pinking, lotus feet
He will reward your love with an embrace
and a smile upon his merciful face
as this army of Cupid meets defeat,
as this lovely Lord and you meet.

Madhava

Vrindavani Dasi

Beware, my friend, of that eastern place
Nadia, ruled by He with the moonlike face.
Do not enter that city on the Ganges' banks
if you fear to join insanity's ranks,
for the people of this land are moonstruck and mad,
enticed and enthralled by that moonfaced lad.

He steals hearts and minds without lifting a hand,
while adorned with jewels He idly stands.
The world is overwhelmed by His sidelong glance;
We discard past present future, lost and entranced.
His theft—it is final; His smile—so sweet.
We will fight thousands of battles to reach His lotus feet.

This masterful, blackish, mischievous Lord
makes you His and then sends you across the world.
Away from my Lord, how can I live?
For a glimpse of His form, what I would give!

So beware, my friends, of that eastern land.
And oh, my friends! run there as fast as you can.
This madness is sadness and the sadness is joy
for it is touched by the smile of that dark-hued boy.

The Bluish Black Boy

Dr. Prachi Desai

In the pastures of Vrindavan
there's a boy: so lovely!

His skin is bluish-black, hair curly.
Some call Him Devaki-Nandan, some Yashomati-Nandan.

His sweet tunes on the flute,
steal the hearts of many.

He can make a mute sing,
and the crippled dance in ecstasy.

His whereabouts are many:
Mathura, Vrindavan, Gokul and Dwarka.

But He especially likes to reside in
the hearts of his beloveds.

Those who love Him purely
do so without a trace of selfishness.

They are His favorite companions:
His mercy flows through them.

From those beautiful green Pastures of Vrindavan,
He's calling us back,
to be with Him,
for all of eternity.

So let's not miss this chance,
of singing and dancing back
to our heart's homeland!!

Resident of My Heart
Priyanka

In my heart he resides,
and in his heart the world resides.

By his soft curly locks of hair
like a ripe black jambula
I am dyed in the deep crimson of his love.
Intoxicated by his charm
and seduced by his smell
I find myself immersed in a spell.

In my heart he resides,
and in his heart the world resides.

My heart dances
to the tunes of his music
and skips a beat
when his silky yellow dhoti
brushes against my red embroidered skirt.

In my heart he resides,
and in his heart the world resides.

Satiated, yet desiring for more,
by the taste of his raspberry-like lips.
The heat from his warm embrace
penetrates through my skin and limbs
and soothes my soul.

May I be locked in his arms forever!

In my heart he resides,
and in his heart I reside…

The Chemist

Sudevi Geary

He opens his chest and I walk in,
waiting for the dark of my eyes to adjust to his light.
He doesn't seem to mind my blindness
soft cool hands find mine, pulling me
through undercurrent corridors,
the wide and narrow waterways of a life
moved along, by a heart driven to beat.

The descent below the surface world
swells through unaccustomed veins, the planets
spun off-course, the dizzying loss of destiny,
and I submerged, as he is, am handed vision of what lies
ahead by choice, a bright opening above all others.

Through the mazes he knows, I'm shown
the path to secret chambers dressed in velvet curtains;
steam of childhood scents, the flavour of our first loves
dancing on marble altars when we turn off the lights.

He lives inside of himself, universes in the making.
Sweet alchemy of the soul gathered in his fingertips.

Burst Open the Doors of My Heart
Vicitri Dasi

You touched my heart so deep inside
You found my soul and made it come alive
"Come out, come out! No more shall you hide
Don't worry—I shall deliver you from indomitable pride."

You embraced my heart tight from within
with your strong arms; and would not release,
and invited me to enter *rasa lila*: to dance and sing
eternally in joy with our Swamini and Her sweetheart.

"You belong here. This is your place.
Why tarry? Don't delay. Give up all else.
Forget your body and all things related.
Sri Yugala are waiting for you. Can't you understand?
They are waiting just for you—for that special delightful
seva that no one else can do,
for your special unique flavor of prema
your delightful way of doing things,
making Them laugh, charming Their hearts
with Your very own expressions of love.
Why continue to deny Them—and yourself?
You are Their property so come home, come home.
You belong in the kunja, decorating with flowers,
spreading your fragrance in the air,
Their pleasure not complete without you.
So why hold out longer? What taste are you getting here?
Remember Gopa Kumara?—How Krishna was so overjoyed
when he finally came to Vraja? Krishna broke through
the weeping crowd to greet and embrace His long-lost friend?

"O Sridama, look! Sarupa has come!" What joy! Finally after millions of births, finally. Krishna ran and embraced him tight and then fainted on the spot – such was His happiness."

Your kumkuma-coated words wafted into my ear
blown along on the Malayan breeze of your soothing voice.
They burst-open the doors of my heart!
Doors that had been tightly shut to any scent of bhakti for
    uncountable eons.
That heart—dark and seething with unmentionable desires—
now under the direction of your sweet smile which
heralded in the waters of Pancha-veni,
washing away fear, remorse, lamentation and sin,
clearing the path for Pancha-tattva and the whole kirtana
    party to enter.
Their joyous singing and dancing immediately filled the
    dark cavern.
Their roaring sound cracked open the cave's thick
    impenetrable walls
allowing in the divine light of Truth, lighting up that
    ancient dark place
and, lo and behold, it transformed into a fragrant
    flowering kunja
filled with the sounds of bees humming, cuckoos and
    peacocks calling from outside,
Yamuna's gurgling waters flowing nearby. And
beautiful Yugala Kishora in the center, lounging on Their
    love-couch
languid after rati-keli, fanned and massaged by Their
    charming *kinkoris*.
Then, one particularly sweet *dasi* placed a *chamara* in my hand
and gave me a place near Them, beckoning me to begin my seva.

Yes, Beti, you have arrived. You are home. Weep no more.

The Dance
Radha Cornia

Madana-mohan moves through the night
To capture the Gopis, hearts beating like drums.
They steal from their homes in secretive flight
To the Lord of their dance, here He comes, O He comes!

The sound of His flute floating softly through the air
As they rush from their homes in complete disarray,
The thought of His countenance, moon-like and fair
Captures their hearts and drags them away.

Proudest of women these friends of Gopal,
Each feels His arms in loving embrace.
Of His devotees most blessed of all,
Those maidens of Vraja who dance with such grace.

Yet blink but one eye and their lover has fled,
They circle alone under moon light and cloud.
They stumble and fall to the ground like the dead
With their grief stricken voices crying aloud.

"O trees, have you seen that most beautiful One,
Whose flute calls us out from our homes in the night?
Creepers, please help us, our hearts are undone,
Govinda may never return to our sight."

Seeking their lover, they find in the earth
The footsteps of Radhika and Nandulal.
"How can we measure the ultimate worth of that Gopi
Whose worship surpasses us all?"

But wearing the crown made by Krishna's own hand
Radha thinks she has outdone all the rest.
Alone with Her lover, She has one demand,
"Carry Me, Krishna," she sweetly requests.

"Climb on My shoulders," Her cowherd commands
And the moon dims its light in the clouds overhead.
Krishna leaves Radha alone in the sand
Radha is stunned and Her heart fills with dread.

Yet in her grief, She awakens to know
Pride in His love was the cause of Her fall
The loss of dear Shyama—an irreparable blow
To one who has given the most love of all.

She bleakly remembers His smile, honey-sweet
Bimba red lips and soft blue-black hair
The thrill of Her heart when Their loving eyes meet
Now the loss of Shyama's glances crowns her despair.

Then like the dawn when the sun's shining rays
Burn like a flame through Vraja's dark night
Krishna appears in a glorious blaze
The glow of His smile the Gopis' delight

The hearts of the Gopis like high standing hills
Drown in the nectar of Krishna's sweet glance
Cool moon lit rays shine down on them still
In the endlessly circling Rasa dance

Step to the left, hand touching hand
Each Gopi ensnared by Krishna's dark eyes
Step to the right across the soft sand
With ankle bells tinkling under dark skies

Madana Mohan moves through the night
To capture the Gopis, hearts beating like drums
They steal from their homes in secretive flight
To the Lord of their dance, here He comes, O He comes!

Darshan

Jai Radhika Devi Dasi

As I walk through an ancient temple,
the sounds of the village beyond the stone walls begin to fade.
I hear the faint sound of a flute sounding at once close and
      yet distant.
I pause on a walkway looking down through an archway
      into a courtyard.

The most exquisite woman I have ever seen dances enticingly,
alone to the sound of the flute.
Her golden bangles add their own accompaniment.
Flower petals float down from the sky to swirl and dance with her.
They ecstatically give up their fragrance as her bare feet
      gently crush them.

As I watch enraptured, I feel a presence behind me.
He places his hand upon my back and together we watch
      her transfixed.
He at once feels solid and of spirit…as of this world and yet not.

As we watch, She looks up…arms and eyes reaching towards us.
She is dancing for Him.
Giving Herself for his pleasure and also drawing Him closer.
An inhale and exhale: The two parts of a single heartbeat.

I feel Her divine love for Him shoot at us like a lightning bolt.
It takes my breath away as it passes through me to Him.
And then just as quickly, I feel Him respond:
His divine love for Her passing through me to Her.
I have never felt anything so powerful.

Even as they disappear before my material eyes;
the sound of the flute, the fragrance of the flowers,
and the divine love
remain in my heart.

Radha

Braja Sorensen

My mind inhales a caravan of painful thoughts,
exhaling them onto the sands of my heart.

I resist, like a gull running at water's edge,
pushing back the tide of memories.

Your words of love crash like stubborn waves
that need to land while morning lasts.

Promises uttered pound at my heart;
I am beached on the shore of yearning.

The wine of love won't stain my lips:
in the chalice of my heart, thirst lies unquenched

and tears stand sentinel to my ardor,
both the ornament and palanquin of grief.

My heart, lined with sorrow, is burdened
with the tyranny of separation;

I am told it is a balm, yet pain is all I know.
Let its bitter taste fill me, then…

I shall bravely swallow the tonic
of the vagrant whose veil shrouds my heart;

I cannot find a surrogate for the trails of poison it leaks
into a heart that longs

for only You

Radha Krishna's Moon

Krishna Vidya Mitchell

Radha wades in the river Yamuna
Krishna's flute echoes in the trees of Vrindavan
The moon's nectar is his eyes turn from
brown to bright blue gazing at her with
devotion so pure the river blooms with lotus
flowers.

She reaches out, and tears of honey flow
and cover her palms. She awakens
with such delight knowing Krishna
is forever one within her, and forever
One without her.

She returns to Vrindavan
sweet with smells of eternal passion
Restlessness be gone!
The Gopis know:
Krishna and Radha are now
One.

CHAPTER THREE

GURU & SANGA

"Show me the others
Who after so many miles
Still are joyful, still dance.
They are the part of you
that reaches out to me and calls me,
Daughter."

Dhanya Rico

Reflections on Guru and Sanga

Dhanya Rico

A guru is a loving guide who selflessly illuminates our path toward Krishna, or God. My personal journey to my relationship with my guru was gradual. It took inner work; finding out what I really wanted to do in this life and how I wanted to proceed in my spiritual practice. Although I had grown up with spiritual texts and activities at my fingertips, as an adult I had to decide if this truly was a path I wanted to commit to.

Our Vaishnava literature explicitly encourages us to be active, not passive; inquisitive and curious, not mindless; and fully exercise our free will, not simply follow the flow of the status quo. In these sacred texts, a guru is described as a person who is fully immersed in their relationship with Krishna, and who inspires and encourages us to do the same.

Likewise, the word guru is sometimes defined as "heavy", indicating that the person—and for that matter the topic—is not taken lightly. Our relationship with our guru is designed to keep us present, engaged and focused. Yet it is not limited by time, space or physical presence. Moreover, and very importantly, guru is such by qualification alone. They are a vessel of spiritual knowledge that is unchanged and timeless.

By opening myself to the idea of being a serious student of that knowledge, I felt that my heart cracked open just enough to let in the warm rays of my guru's kindness. I took great comfort in the fact that my guru is truly absorbed in God consciousness, and that he expressed eagerness that I take up that same work. I was not only awed by his capacity as a spiritual teacher, but by his dedication as a student of his own guru.

A hesitation I often hear, and one I have had myself, is the acceptance of a guru at the cost of our own individuality or uniqueness. Will I lose myself in this relationship? This worry not only points to our innate desire for spirituality characterized by a personal relationship but also to the deep knowing that our uniqueness is valuable: a gift!

In my own experience—and that of many others with whom I have conversed on this topic—a dedicated relationship with guru allows for clearer distinction between the essential and the nonessential in our lives. This means that someone whose sole interest is your spiritual wellbeing helps you to identify what is truly important and then warmly encourages you to pursue it without hesitation. This natural affection is a necessary component because the relationship itself is a space for trust and growth. With this clarity, my uniqueness, my service, begins to surface and give meaning to my life. In this way, my relationship with guru highlights and enhances my individuality.

Interestingly, one of the most essential teachings transmitted by guru is also that all souls are equal in spiritual quality and worth. Designations of race, age, gender, class, religion, etc. are non-spiritual and therefore, nonessential. Neither guru nor disciple is limited by these categories and therefore he/she encourages us to develop this equal vision and expand it to our relationship with all beings.

Recognition of our unity with all beings can create a deep shift within us and also in our relationships, or *sanga*. Rather than highlighting our differences—perhaps as a means of clinging to our seemingly threatened uniqueness—we are able to recognize all the ways in which we are the same. We can recognize the universality of struggle in this world, and the soul's unending quest for love. From this place, our actions can be based in compassion and our relationships can become areas of spiritual practice in and of themselves.

Sanga, is defined as "coming together": a joining. When engaging with another, we set into motion experiences that will call on our ability to simultaneously acknowledge our individuality and our unity. Paying attention to aspects as seemingly small as our body language, we begin this practice by turning each interaction we have in a relationship—or within our community—into opportunities to enact the instructions and mood of our spiritual teachers. As such, it begins to govern our language, our treatment of one another, our disposition toward those who perceive as similar to us, and especially our treatment toward those who we perceive as different.

We then begin to see our partners, friends, family, and community members not only as beautiful, unique beings but also as dynamic reflections of where we are at in our own spiritual journey. By developing relationships rooted in this intention, we will cultivate close, trusting bonds, allowing us to reveal our thoughts and feelings in confidence with another, and reciprocate that. The relationships become a way to lovingly gauge the aspects of ourselves that we can further develop in pursuit of the humble mood of our teachers: to become the servant of the servant, of the servant of God.

This mood of humility and sincerely offering respect onto others is the prime qualification to unite, most authentically, in glorification of God. Whether we are joining together to chant the Maha Mantra or share spiritually inspiring poetry, it requires a great deal of vulnerability to sit and truly open your heart in this way. The creation of sacred spaces wherein this inspiration can be expressed and shared—as in this book—is essential in developing authentic *sanga*.

When we invite another to reveal their deepest feelings with us and hold these with care as a matter of spiritual importance, that is *sanga*. The only way we will be able to help grow the devotion of current practitioners, and inspire those who are curious about our spiritual tradition, will be to work fervently to provide an atmosphere of trust: one where we can each feel completely free and encouraged to offer our hearts, minds, and words to the Supreme Lord, Sri Krishna.

Show Me the Others

Dhanya Rico

I want to be awake in my choices
Contemplate
Move, work, speak
With whole heart and lit mind.
Words steeped in thought.
Eyes well read
Trained on the pages you have so
Lovingly filled with
Knowing.

If you are who I think you are
You wish this for me
As much as I wish it for myself.
You have cleared the path
So I may joyfully dance upon it.
Show me the others
Who in your footsteps follow
On whose breath
Timeless songs of Truth are sung.

Show me the others
Who after so many miles
Still are joyful, still dance.
They are the part of you that reaches out to me and calls me,
Daughter.

Vaikuntha Man

Mandali Dasi

Oh, dear friend,
Vaikuntha man,
Vicious is Providence's plan!

I yearn the day will soon be mine
When my paper cage
I will burn away.

Then I will be free to roam
The holy village in my loving form
And really serve my fellow friends
Without the cloudy matter dress.

Hope is there that in the end,
Vaikuntha man will help his friend.

Temple of Gratitude

Madhava Lata Devi Dasi

In many ways
I could sing
my gratitude to you,
the words could be
written on leaves
to be blown every day in the wind
as a prayer;
or I could incise with gratitude
barks and woods
as mementoes, reminding me
how much I owe you;
or I could engrave my gratitude
in gold
like the love for the Lord
you gave us, that you spoke tirelessly of,
or I could mould my gratitude
in bronze
to make it strong, unfailing
as the shelter you gave;
I could also sculpt it in marble,
white like the purity and faith
that made you a warrior
without stains;
or I could take
the wood, the marble, the gold and all,
and with them inlay
the wall
of my temple of gratitude,
to endure time,
like the certitude,

you've instilled in our souls,
of a spiritual world;
But I have a stony heart
what could I do?
Since you see only the good
in whatever one has,
I carved in there, in stone
my gratitude.

Even heart-shaped stones
last forever
and certainly—whenever,
can convey a message of love.

A Cry in the Night

Rukmini Walker

Lying awake
On a Delhi night
A watchman's stick pounds out his plight:

"O Ram! Ram! Ram! Ram!"
And a howling dog whines,
"How long? How long?,
O Lord and Master,
When will You answer?"

And how do I cry from the deepest place?
And how does one come to attract Your grace?

O Prabhupada,
Please accept me!
And please be pleased
To recommend me!

To the One Who steals the heart
And all the Gopis' butter pots,
And to Sri Radha,
His dear-most lover.

O Hari! O Hara!
Please pity my plight,
And steal my heart,
Like a thief in the night.

A Labor of Love
Omika Mali

Dearest Grandfather,
I ask myself everyday
How can I serve you?
Please show me the way

Dearest grandfather,
How can I give?
I feel a fire swelling up in my heart
What is the way this life is meant to be lived?

I can't turn a page without tears in my eyes
When I read about you, I just want to cry
How did you leave on the Jaladutta with no ties?
How did you forsake wealth, comfort, and sanctity without
even a proper goodbye?

Suffering a heart attack
You came to the West for me
Giving Krishna to my parents, and my guru
So one day I could experience the ecstatic mellows of Bhakti

When I think about your struggle
And the man who almost slashed you with a knife
I get ferociously angry
How did you deal with such hatred, and lust without any strife?

Your life is a lesson
On the power of suffering to teach
You accepted every single setback you went through
With intense humility

You suffered three heart attacks on the Jaladutta ship
Suffering so much to come to the United States
Only such a man with a heart of gold
Can forsake comfort, to come and preach so bold!

I wish I could have beheld
Your great presence with my small eyes
I wish I could have felt
Your instructions cutting my ego with a knife

But though you are far away
I lie awake tonight
Feeling you plant a seed in my heart
Feeling you cut my attachments to worldly sights
I can't sleep, or eat
I feel suffocated by the flames of longing in my heart
I want to serve your lotus feet
My life is married to your mission, they will never be apart.

Prabhupada, I've never met you
We've never had the opportunity to speak
But why is this calling so strong?
Why does it make my knees so weak?

I think it's the power of your love
Imparted to me through my guru and my parents alike
I may not know you personally

But I still feel like your mission of God consciousness
has given me life

It is my responsibility to not let your sacrifices go in vain
I'm a grandchild born and bred by the village of ISKCON
To let this mission dwindle
Would be insane

Dearest granddad, I see your project
And it has wounds in its arms, legs and thighs
Would you be happy with the International Society for
Krishna Consciousness today?
Would you be smiling as you heard its wailing cries?

And so, granddad I deeply pray
"Please reveal to me how to use this life?"
You almost died to give me the precious gems of bhakti
I have to fight this war against Maya for you!
No more being polite!

Fight Arjuna! Fight Arjuna!
It's a call to arms!
How are we fighting for Prabhupada?
How are we revealing Bhakti's charms?

Fight Arjuna! Fight Arjuna!
Why are we so weak even though we are so young?
Don't we know we've been left with a legacy?
The holy name in every town and village must be sung!

And so as I lay awake, staring at my white roof alone
I pray, "Prabhupada reveal my service, as now I am grown!"

My life is yours, dearest grandfather, make me dance as you please
And though I am weak and flawed, make me someone who sees

That Krishna's love is everywhere, and now it is my duty to give
Prabhupada I am yours, use my tiny life to live
I am full of ecstasy as I surrender to your lotus feet
I am a small child, simply begging for your mercy!

And with this prayer, I finally depart to sleep
Tossing and turning as my inner flames devour me
Though I am impatient, I will wait as my calling manifests slowly
My life is a labor of love, to the granddad I love so dearly!

A Life with Purpose
Gandarvika Devi Dasi

Sundays with Dad in the park:
Loud music, shaved heads, festival tent, seed planted.
Faded mental impressions of a five-year old.

Ponytails in the airport.
Trip to grandma's:
Spiritual books with beautiful pictures for a dollar.

Summer beach nights.
Wandering monk in orange with hands full:
Sweet bars and magazines, again beautiful pictures.

High school adventures and risks
Hare Krishna temple love feast!
Crazy people, crazy clothes and strange food.

Late teen—early adult suffering
Work, school, parties…repeat.
Then, one "life changing" party:
Met a devotee and your Bhagavad Gita.

More Bhagavad Gita, more Bhagavad Gita, less parties.
More devotees, more books, more love feasts, less suffering.
Hey! What's that on the altar?

Beginning to feel bound by philosophy:
Feeling some relief, feeling a new life coming on:
Ashrama bed…early mornings, living the books.

Years of friends, family and festivals:
Deepest love ever felt.
Riding the wave of service and spiritual abundance.

I've changed bodies within my body.
Experienced life like never imagined:
Been places, met people, learned things I never dreamed of.

Not always easy, not always hard:
Learning to give instead of take
Always with purpose and showers of love.

Took on a new life, gave a new life,
shared a life with amazing souls.
Relationships planted, fertilized: I valued all.

What a journey! What a life!
So much mercy received, so much gained!
So much more to come my way.

Five years old, fifteen years old, and 'till now
I owe all to you, Srila Prabhupada:
Your disciples, your books, your temples, your words.

My story is the story of many before me, and those yet to come.
Now, please help us plant the seed of mercy in others,
    as you did for us:
Through books, temples, sweet balls, love and purpose.

Living a purposeful life undeserved. *Why me?*
Only because of you.

Prayers to the Guru

Vrindavanesvari Aguilera

To obtain Krishna *prem*, love of Godhead pure
The lotus feet of our guru, the only method sure
With great awe and reverence, at his lotus feet I bow
The sea of material suffering, to cross it, but how?
The spiritual master's grace is the vessel that we need
Krishna's mercy obtainable if his advice one does heed

To have my consciousness cleansed is my one true goal
Words from his lotus lips purify my heart and soul
Fulfilled are all of one's wishes and notions
If you attach to his lotus feet with perfect devotion

My eyes were dark and blind, my heart empty and dull
Now my vision's clear and bright, my heart transcendentally full
My Lord, he is, through the cycles of death and rebirth
From him, supreme happiness flows, true spiritual mirth
Ignorance he dispels, pure knowledge he does bring
Of his character and glories, the Vedic scriptures do sing

Lord and master of the devotees, benefic friend of the poor
Our spiritual master's mercy can fill an ocean and more
Be merciful unto me, oh master so kind
The shade of your lotus feet is the only shelter I find
All over the three worlds, your fame is duly spread
At your lotus feet, I lay my worthless head

(A poetic rendition of Srila Narottam Das Thakura's 'Sri Guru-Vandana' translated prayers)

The Importance of the Spiritual Master

Krishna Priya Dasi

This life is full of miseries,
Full of contention and discord.
Asking ourselves why this is,
We find our questions ignored.

Our desire tree has many branches,
Which takes our peace of mind.
We jump from branch to branch,
But what we seek, we cannot find.

Drowning in the ocean of mundane affairs,
We're helpless without any strength.
And devoid of a spiritual master's guidance,
It's not possible to cross this ocean's length

The spiritual master is that one person
To introduce us to the Lord.
Without the shelter of his lotus feet,
Our human life is completely deplored.

The generous mercy of his Holiness
Is giving initiation and instruction.
Trying to fix our flickering minds on Krishna,
He leads us to devotional perfection.

The shower head is a god I talk to

Pranada Comtois

as I lose touch with my hair, skin, bones
swim in the waters
of lessons taught by many masters

my favorite Prabhupada

by whom I go deeper into the wisdom
of all the other teachers

a wild daisy
an orange-pink sunset on clouds
the exhale-breath that closes my eyes
a tree that lost a limb
rapid-succession-deaths of friends
a hummingbird milking a firecracker bush
the knife-cut map lines on my stomach.

Gurudev

Aradhana Devi Dasi

Gurudev,
Your guidance is a gift that I'm growing more gratitude
    for everyday.
You are the embodiment of my faith by grace,
In the unsteadiness, I always know that you are there.
I am able to look up from my low position and see your
    hand reaching out
an appearance side by side with Gaura
not looking at my past
but looking at what you both see as hope
to receive the nourishment to hold on
by drinking from the lake of the Goswamis
faithfully following your guidance.
This *parivara* of Bhaktivinoda
a path that echoes with the roars
smelling of the petal remnants
painted with affection
to garland the world—
In you
I see the heavy conviction of Bhaktivinode
In you
I see the love that urged Bhaktisiddanta to pull the mosquito
    nets over his disciples while they were sleeping
In you
I see the humble confidence that held the spine of Bhaktivedanta
In you
I see the external simplicity, the eternal heart woven in
    between the lines

of the Bhagavatam and between the fingers of
    Nityananda Prabhu
of Bhaki Raksaksa Sridhara Maharaja
In you
I see my only hope.
A hope that I'm building gratitude for everyday.

The Transcendental Sadhu
Devarsi Radhika Devi Dasi

Dissipating
Darkness, Your grace spoke,
Of *japa's* potency vast

Rekindling,
Godhead's love, it stroke
Heart's deepest chords, at last

Dedicated
To Srila Prabhupada, you led
The life of a transcendental *sadhu*

Harmonious,
Is the path you tread,
Pure as a fresh lotus' dew

Compassionate,
Towards fallen souls, you bestow
Your love and kindness to proceed

Establishing,
My faith, you then plough,
My heart to sow the seed.

Grateful
Hence, is the lost child that saw
That beam of spiritual moonlight.

Indebted,
She remains, with awe
Towards that guiding knight.

Harikatha

Sudevi Geary

In the cove of this rainbow
you explode sun blinding
love through our walls
burning urban sanctuary
dissipating grey
with diamonds falling
from your maddened roof;
these compassionate skies
cook us
butter on your words
bathe me under
the glance of your Truth.

Just for a Moment

Gopi Kumari Devi Dasi

A glance,
just for a moment,
fills our hearts with eternal joy...

Sweet words,
however short,
warm our hearts forever...

Your grace,
and kindness,
limitlessly permeate our hearts...

Your smile,
your laughter,
have us longing for you to be near...

Jaya Gurudeva!

Lion Heart

Mallika Dasi Somershein

Sometimes many tests come to assail us
and we feel there are none to avail us
of the epic movie battle going on inside:
our private screening we choose to hide.
Our mind says one thing, our heart another:
Which is which? We then start to wonder.
Going back and forth with justifications
while outwardly looking for explanations.

Sometimes a storm is needed for us to seek shelter,
other times we choose to grunt and bear the weather.
But then we learn the necessity of carrying an umbrella,
and on our heads, take His instructions as our agenda.

Over and over we are tempted by Maya's ploys
as our mental diseases attempt to destroy us.
But simultaneously, Gurudeva extends his hand
with assuring words, he says: "Yes, I understand"
Anguishes of the mind, slammed into our face
are the real extensions of Sri Guru and his grace.
They give us the chance to cry out in pain,
the sincerity to reach the spiritual plane

He Gurudeva, He Gurudeva! He Gurudeva!

In heart you have already installed a lion encaged
which—if fed properly—becomes completely enraged
ripping to shreds all types of elephantine qualities:
the ultimate shelter and protector of all devotees.

So with a lion heart I move forward, strong and brave,
calling: "*He Prabhu! He Chaitanya! He Narashimhadeva!*

Your cub is now learning how to have strong faith:
how to roar—as You do—to keep me sound and safe.
No fear from endless temptations, or Hiranyakasipus
for I take shelter of Your mercy, to do as You would do.

The Opening of My Heart

Tulasi Kunja Devi Dasi

My life as of late
Is defined by my spine.
A new kind of strength,
How it curves and extends…
It permits me to fight
Beyond the scope of my skin,
"Not concerned with
the external superficialities
of anything."

A flower—bloomed,
Now used
To string my bow.
Drenched,
In this essence,
Is where your spine
Supports mine.

And even if no one sees,
There is an awareness, of pressure,
Like wind is to air.

Your heart—my most reverenced form of growth.
Fascinated by the properties of our non-conditional nature.
Even in decomposition,
You manage to see
The ways we are built up.
An ongoing conversation,
You listen to everything,
To revive the ways we know.

Because in nature,
There is a system of subtleties
Not concerned with the perceived
Imperfections
Of the ways that matter
Wages war.
Nature is not concerned
With your ligaments
Or tectonic breaks, or
Skeletal derails.

In decomposing the structure
You've taught me to nurture
The margins of our gardens
The momentary pulsations
Between every meeting of the two,
The rhythms that blossom
From the silence in the spaces,
The movement in the stillness
Where our eternal beloved blooms.

My Soul Savior

Akarsini Radhika Devi Dasi

I humbly prostrate at my savior's lotus feet,
I beg, and pray, and cry
to remain there eternally.
Traveling the globe for world purification
nothing can stop his determination.
He makes divine joy and love
dance in people's heart.
Having made Srila Prabhupada
the worshipable deity of his heart.
Through insurmountable hurdles,
he is showing the world what is worthy to behold:
"Not the body as a whole! But Radha, Krishna and Nitai Gaur!
Are the only life for all."
He is fighting, steady and strong,
for the benefit of all.
And whoever stands by him
attains joy from deep within.
Oh! Blessed are those he glances upon,
and those who his prayers get;
As they will indeed get caught
in Lord Gauranga's sankirtan net.
And, for me—this helpless soul—I grab his lotus feet
Recognizing they are my only reason to live.

Living Still, In Sound

Jahnavi Harrison

Today the sky is scudded with clouds,
and the paperboy trudges to house after house,
delivering the news of the day.
The headlines reveal little to celebrate.
You could be forgiven for thinking
this is just an ordinary, November Sunday morning.
But somewhere in the distance, drums are being beaten.
No poppy wreaths are laid, but flower garlands are hung
          across doors and shoulders,
and rose and marigold petals fly through the air!
Bells ring, cutting through the chatter with a herald of celebration.
And thousands upon thousands, bow to the ground—
with gratitude that you ever walked this troubled earth.
Oh my glorious grandfather,
you are living still in sound,
in image, word and instruction, your light remains undimmed.
Your urgent message only grows in relevance,
with each turning of the day.
You have given all the answers,
the goal, the process and the path,
please help me follow truly now, and serve you day by day.

Connection

Krishna-mayi Dasi

My spiritual family is special in many ways.
Gurudeva is the like the sunshine, you all are like the rays.

Each one of us is a piece, of a puzzle that is quite large.
Different natures and *sevas*, and knowing Gurudeva is
    always in charge.

Binding us together, is our beloved holy master.
Whom without, our lives, would be a complete and utter disaster.

Srila Gurudeva planted something special in each of our hearts.
Fascinating to see the uniqueness of each and every part.

How many times did we hear, to not quarrel or criticize?
Those bad qualities will come into us, he would always advise.

On a daily basis, I'm surrounded by those without
    transcendental knowledge.
So the devotees' purity, goodness, and kindness, is easy
    to acknowledge.

"You must help start this revolution," Gurudeva once told to me.
How? That's impossible! I'm just anger-filled, not even a devotee.

Starting to get a glimpse, seventeen years later:
To help others learn about Krishna, with love, there is
    nothing greater.

Yet it's so hard to be strong, without physically being
    recharged by you.
Just being in your presence gray skies quickly turned to blue.

All miseries, upsetness, difficulties vanished away.
Like a magician, you made us only want to hear, chant, and pray.

Without your coming to this world we would all be bereft.
Stealing our hearts and minds, unlimited emptiness when you left.

Sweet nectar, like tonic, your Hari-*katha* would pour into our ears:
Entering hearts, relinquishing all of our fears.

Delivering the *jivas* of the world, you are the most precious jewel.
Assuming the position of spiritual master, giving us
    meaning to life and fuel.

Eternally residing in Vraja, completely immersed in bliss.
Granting the entrance to Their service, a chance we cannot miss.

To the reservoir of unconditional compassion, I pray at
    your lotus feet.
Please give me refuge eternally, and keep me close, until
    we again meet.

CHAPTER FOUR

OUR SELVES & OTHERS

*When You and I can talk again
face to face, as in the lasting land.
When You and I take time again
to remind me who I am.*

JANAVI HELD

Our Relationships with Our Selves and Others

Urmila Devi Dasi

Who are we? Our body grows in the womb and we enter the world with a ready-made identity as someone's child, a gender, a nationality. The various identities we clothe ourselves in—based on a mix of fashionable tastes that we, and others, gradually cultivate—solidify to define our sense of self. But, are we truly any of these?

The *Bhagavad Gita* and all eternal wisdom—indeed, our own introspective experience—tells us that we are a spiritual being whose "I" has merely a most fleeting connection with all those external identities. And, as we are beyond the mundane, so is all life around us. All the "others" are transcendent entities as well. We are connected as parts of our common source: an all-pervading, divine person who is everywhere and in everything.

Only when we awaken to our relationship with our source do we truly connect with both ourselves and others. Additionally, we find the true residence for the various temporary identities that create the illusion of worldly duties, and we offer those to Krishna, our source, out of love.

The poems in this chapter reflect our understanding of our real self—the spiritual and eternal—to whatever extent we have awakened to that reality. They also delve into how we love others, or attempt to love them, as our sense of our authentic relationship with them unfolds. But our dealings with ourselves, and others on the illusory platform—this is my mother, my child, my sister, my enemy—are also touched upon here. After all, until we are fully free, those identities and relationships are a large part of our story. They provide the framework upon which we paint the canvas of this brief life, and are often the springboard from which we dive into the clear pool of spirituality.

The *Bhagavatam* and the *Bhagavad Gita* insist that identity and relationships be the foundation for all else—material and spiritual. Relishing and rejoicing in ourselves, neutrality towards friends and enemies, freedom from envy, and kindness toward every living being, are all essential on the spiritual path. As we read these poems, we empathize with the struggles and heartbreak and soar with the epiphanies of the poets. Our thoughts, hearts, and hands unfold the budding flower and fruit of our soul.

Who Am I?

Tivra-bhakti Devi Dasi

Looking into the mirror
Wondering
Who am I?
Am I this breathing *yantra*,
which changes weight and height,
which drops a part
—amputated leg, a tooth—
maintaining still something same?
Am I that weight or part,
or is it mine?

I would be pleased to meet
the part which I could call "me"

My Dear Inner Critic
Gopika-kanta Dasi

My dear Inner Critic,
You told me that other people know the way,
And if I didn't listen to them, I would pay.

You told me that opinions were gold,
That if I had more of them, I *would* be bold.

You told me that about me, nobody cared…
that trust in this world was truly rare.

But my dear Inner Critic, I am happy to say you were wrong!
I found a voice in my heart, singing a song!

That voice reminds me that I must trust,
Remembering others love me is a must.

The voice reminds me of how much I have been blessed
Even if I feel some needs have not been addressed.

My dear Inner Critic, I am telling you today,
that we must always remember to quietly pray…

Because when we feel scared, not knowing where to lay…
God will always be there to show us the way.

Far Away from Goloka

Yasomati Devi Dasi

Alas, oh, desert like, oh, empty hearted heart,
Where is the spring of water bringing life to you?
The water-wallah lost the path again
And here you are, with nothing else to do
Than just to dry up, and die a death of sand.
I hope and pray that you will understand
That life and joy just come and go like wind.
Don't put your trust in things that have an end
Just go back home and you will find your spring.

When

Janavi Held

Whenever the future finds me
when memory is gone
when longing no longer reminds me
that remaining here is wrong.

When the night tells me
that all this romance is done
when all along I've known You
and memory is long.

When air-castles lose their altitude
when roaming the moors of time
when I am lost in attitude
thinking everything is mine.

When You and I can talk again
face to face, as in the lasting land
when You and I take time again
to remind me who I am.

When memory goes out walking
out in the fields of time
when I make my life for Your liking
and can't remember what is mine.

When oceans lose their salt
and I am swimming deep
in the autumn twilight, staying
where I can no longer sleep.

When all the world around me
does not resemble time
when souls animate the foundry
of this everlasting ride.

Inner Quest

Jennieke Janaki

Every time we use the mind
trying to find the answers of Life,
the inner quest for everlasting safety,
a deep longing for belonging,
we get so overwhelmed
the mind shuts down.

Only more separation!
Every word or thought we are not anymore
What am I or what are you?

The eternal changing moment
of this realization
Our truthful security:
Only in the loss of time
when we surrender the ego-based desires
will the I in you and me find the comforting Harbor
in the eternal Stillness of Oneness
that comes from Divine Love.

Bless Them
Gopalpreet Taya Malakian

The stores are filled
with books
on how to relate to one another,
how to relate to ourselves.
I have read my share
believe me,
but what the masters say
is true.
Whether you love someone,
hate someone
or feel nothing for someone,
bless them.
Bless them
no matter what.
Bless them when you most resist it.
Bless them with no strings attached.
It is far more effective
and far less complicated
than reading all the books.

Surgeon's Tools

Janavi Held

I wish I had something to give You,
something that would surprise You
and make You smile, but today
You are my surgeon, for I am ill
sick with the disease of eons
transmigrated bacteria
tears at my bones, and You
are my only medicine.

Occasionally, I have the strength
to bring You dirt from my garden,
dead leaves, or discarded shells
mostly I offer my titanic sorrow,
the address of orphaned tears,
or the publicist of my arrogance.
That arrogance, wrapped up
against my heart, shouts and swells
but cannot remember
the embarrassing lessons of yesterday.

I have been vigilant like a thief
stealing away from You at night
and in the dawn I return
with shattered and burning fingers
from cavorting kindly with my enemies.
As I slip by You
into my silent bed
I hear Your surgeon's tools
rattling in the dawn shadows.

Taking Out the Tumors
Gopi Gita Schomaker

A brahmin thread is tied on his wrist
A gift from Sri Govinda's broad chest
"Keep him protected.. Hold him gently."
As they manipulate the material elements.

He was peaceful, equipoised, totally calm,
I kept waiting for his anxiety or upset.
"No, I'm totally fine, don't worry, Mom."
Inner strength on the hospital bed.

A cotton gown, closed and snapped,
A thin foam mattress on wheels,
Bright lights in stylish lanterns wrapped,
The whole place is quite surreal.

The best of facilities all around,
Dr. Angela Price is the neurosurgeon,
One of the top 5 in this town,
Brisk, confident, she strides in.

The surgical team explains every detail,
The where's, the why's, and the how's,
The possible wins and possible fails.
Moving the brain pieces, lotta wows.

Minds comforted, it's a logical start,
Both he and I breathe sighs of relief,
But the real Doctor protects from in his heart,
Removing all fear and there's been no grief!

He has his cell phone, charged it all night,
Asking for his "great-grandfather's" song,
Srila Prabhupada's voice bringing light,
Nurses agreed, took the singing phone along.

Time to go now. They unhook the gurney,
Wait! Sri Nrsimha! His *kavacha* I must say!
Hands on his head, I pray for this journey,
Dear Lord, let her hands not slip or stray.

Powerful Vaishnavas are showing affection,
Prabhupada's right hand men are calling,
Auspiciousness is in all directions,
There really is no need for bawling.

As the sedative starts, his eyes close,
This mom's heart skips a beat,
This smart boy of 15 is my life and soul.
Oh mind, take shelter of Shyam's lotus feet.

They wheel him away, he's gone for now,
6 hours with updates every hour,
We're fortunate you're all with us somehow,
Giving us your spiritual power.

Song to Self

Dhanya Rico

Child,
Take it slow.
Life is a balance
Of troubles and triumphs so…

Just try your best.
Trust in yourself,
You've got what it takes
To be great.

Keep your faith
Rooted in love
Of those who encourage your growth.

Don't hold back
Give it your all.
The whole world is waiting so…

Go.
And when you're singing out
You will know
The truth is inside of you.

Go.
And when you're singing out
You will hear
That She has been calling you
Home.

I Have Been Unmade

Janavi Held

I have been unmade
scattered bits of self
long to be reunited

I long to walk
to feel the elements
spiraling around me

Oh my Lords
this world
this world

there is beauty
You the most
perfect artist

but in this place
in this land of the
temporary

there is also such
ugliness
You create beauty

and as we turn and turn
body to body
life to life

tangled, shrouded
in endless reactions

we create the ugly
things of this world

in a tangle of reactions
I am caught
thick ropes

I cannot cut
I place this bound body
at Your feet

Praying daily
for Your mercy
for Your glance upon

my invisible life

Love most strong
that eternal remedy
I pray will enter my heart

and in that vacuous space
a renaissance will bloom
a transcendental spring

sacred water nourishing
sacred sound
will harvest

vast fields of flowers
to pick and offer
again and again

at Your feet

Healing the Breaks

Ananda Vrindavan Devi

We talk a lot
about perfection
but we really need
to talk a lot
about being broken
broken is the normal
and we can live with that
be happy with that
start from there

We are broken
on so many levels
and that is ok

Then we can go
for healing
for compassion
to the sacred teachings
of the great master, Sri Chaitanya

forever broken, forever healed
it's such a good place to be

Let Them Flow

Atmesvari Dasi

Tears are rivers
that take us to places
majestic, yet simple;
To our one true essence.
They cleanse our soul
and bring us back
from the hidden dungeons
of forgetfulness.
They call our inner child,
remind us of our pressures.
So let them flow.
Feel them roll…
Clearing off the makeup
we put on for show.

Breathe, Baby, Breathe

Jvalamukhi Devi Dasi

Once a wise woman said to me:
"Breathe baby, breathe!
If you try to run away from it
it comes back eventually.
So baby breathe, baby breathe!"

Now she'd been through the worst of it—
those things people never, never see:
the bad, the worse, the unspeakable,
her trauma buried deep, buried deep.

She asked me how I fared today,
I said, Oh, not too poorly.
Though my faith's been tested just yesterday:
three friends, one crash, more tragedy…
just one more tragedy.

Why do we go on?
Thwarted in every way?

"No", she said, "It's not like that!
Life's not meant for suffering
I'm convinced of it!
We are just here to learn.
So baby breathe, baby breathe."

I am spirit soul…never shall I grow old.
And now we are deep, deep, deep, in the love Divine:
I am His, and He is mine, and we are
deep, deep, deep in the love Divine.

The Gold in the Summer
Anuradha Sakhi Devi Dasi

I have splashed in the blue sea
Felt the warmth
In my child's laughter
I am rich in hugs
In the life giving sun
I've felt peace in the ocean
The cheer in a marriage
The colors and sparks in the evening sky
The majesty of the cliffs
But the deepest call of the heart
Has to be
You
When I saw you
I slipped into song
Begging you to accept the wealth of this heart
My little world
Because the gold in the summer
Is you
Your arms reached out
Scattering kindness
We knew your song by heart
And sang it as best we might
Papa, mama, babies
I've been here before
As the child
All there seems to be is singing
The only 'together' that's real
The love we covet and crave
The gold in the summer
That's You…

This love will endure
If bathed in its light…
It's not a crime to love those we do
It's the pain of loss which cripples
Let us sing dear lord,
Let this light shine bright
In doing so may we find Your grace
In those we love
May our heart's connections be safe
Beautified by the gold in the summer
The song
That's You

Pushkar Camel Festival

Rambhoru Devi Dasi

White Sadhus
Walking at sunrise
Through oceans of animal bodies

Camels, bullocks, horses, goats.
Piles of goober, wood and hay.
Carts, turbans, earrings, hookahs

Squatting men around small fires,
Wrinkled faces,
Broken teeth.

Rajastanis watching Europeans
Taking photos of what to them is ordinary
They are not romantic about their nomad style

The Sadhus appreciate
Simplicity and natural living.
The Camel people
Look longingly at watches and cameras.

There is much in common
Between the saintly and the simple
Sleep under the stars.
No frills. Few possessions.

Early morning rising.
Wandering town to town
Rice, dahl, rotis
Greetings of, "Jai Sri Rama"

A saint prefers simplicity
The simple know nothing else.

The Witness

Radha Sundari Devi Dasi

In this one flickering moment of eternal time
I stand witness to the experience unfolding before me:
This drama projected out upon the chessboard of material life,
where I see each person playing his or her part in the cosmic dance,
moving hither and thither by goodness, passion or ignorance,
fighting for, or fleeing from, the face of God,
remembering or forgetting Her, invoking or revoking Him,
inspired by choices made with
a free will that lingers on delicate lotus stems,
just inches between the dirt that bore them
and the fragrance of God's beauteous flowered creation.
And as I strive to understand the steps each one is taking,
again I am reminded that this is all it is: an experience.
The karmic fruit of millions of lifetimes
encapsulated in a learning experience,
The lesson of which is always the same:
Love of God...
By God, with God, from God, to God, for God, in God and
      through the love of God.
And as I watch in silent witness,
I reconnect with the Hand of God
without which not a blade of grass moves.
Feel that loving touch upon my head,
and see in the periphery of my vision,
the mercy of that Hand outstretched to every dancer
in the form of His devotees,
and how that Hand reached out and gently brought our
      son to land:
Falling, not *from* the roof of a six story building,
But directly *into* a pool of grace!

Sprung from the heart of God and the unconditional love
 of the Vaishnavas.
And I melt, as tears of awe and eternal gratitude merge into
 those life-giving, life-saving waters.

And so it is, and it is so.

Vaidiki

Mandali Dasi

Her voice bell-like and deep
dances in our ears
calling attention to Krishna.
Cascading through layers
of unspoken prayers
it moves in our hearts.

Oh, His names are her only treasure.

A prayer for mercy,
a wonderful victory—a flower graced a winter day.

To Mother Indrani

Raga Swan

In our final days together,
I looked upon your face:
a slightly wrinkled, but regal beauty,
displaying all of the Lord's good grace.

Then Krishna came and took you to Him
guiding you gently all the while,
co-creating a glorious leaving,
which, like your life, was full of dignified style.

See, you constantly met and gathered the devotees,
making us your number one priority.
In fact, you phoned and traveled wide to meet us,
totally abandoning your nonsense TV.

Your walker was probably the busiest
often on the edge of the altar.
And why on earth wouldn't it be?
Krishna knew you were a soul who wouldn't falter.

Please pave a way for me to join you,
for you're with guru, I know it's true.
And like all of our earthly pastimes
there will still be so much service to do!

You lived a real and fearless life
perfectly showing the way to Godhead,
that's why this poem is so full of verbs
'Cause actually you're alive, you're not dead.

Of course your Jagannath & Gopal deities will miss you
Almost as much as us,
because you shared Them with us so generously
and over Them, always made such a big fuss.

Thanks for keeping Gurudeva's letters to you
and sharing them with the likes of me,
thanks for garlanding his pictures everyday
because you had the power to see.

I always miss and treasure you Mother Indrani
for making a pure devotion Tsunami.
Your personal ways were a treat to behold
may your next chapters of existence splendidly unfold!

Reunion

Mandie Howard

I stand at the gravestone of yesterday's bliss
There's nothing buried here but something's amiss
The war that we wage is the war that we lose
But sometimes the peaceful path isn't easy to choose

We rage with the fire and we ram like the buck
Pull up our roots where the lightning has struck.

And I lost you
And you lost me
In the battle clouds of smoke where we couldn't see
That being right or being wrong wasn't worth being free

The casualties and the victories are one and the same,
For the blood spilled to draw the line bears every one's name.

Some day our scars will be one with the rest
We'll wash away the bloodstains and clean up the mess

We'll reckon our love and make our way to the fields
Where we'll reset the wares of our hearts finest yields

And I lost you
And you lost me
Our retreat went silently, into the trees,
where we could fall down and grieve

Marching our own paths we are eternally entwined
Still laughing in the stars, troubles shed far behind

Our muskets and powder with the cold bayonet
Will be overgrown by the garden's gate where we first met

We'll be welcomed home as though we never left to rejoin our kin
All the souls that God has ever made…together again.

And I'll find you
And you'll find me
Eternally, eternally, eternally

Vaisnava Farewell

Jahnavi Harrison

The sun will rise soon, throw off your sleep,
Today we will celebrate, we shall not weep,
Leave your houses as bells resound,
Let the drums and cymbals be heard all around.

Let unseen airplanes circle above,
Let them gather to hear our offerings of love
Hang fragrant garlands around each door
Give rice in hand to the young and poor

The shore bears witness as we honor you today,
May our prayers be your ferry as the ocean gives way
You have nothing to fear as you leave this place,
Run now, run to his waiting embrace!

CHAPTER FIVE

MAYA'S MAGIC

There are illusionary dreams
that entangle me with this world.
And there is a real dream
that drives me toward You.
I long to dream *that* dream!

CHAMPAK MANJARI DASI

Krishna's Illusive and Divine Potencies

Visakha Dasi

What is *maya*? Most often, Srila Prabhupada—my Guru Maharaja and the person who first introduced the Bhakti tradition to the Western world—translates *maya* as 'illusion' or "that which is not." But he also says, "there is another meaning of *maya*—that is, 'causeless mercy'. There are two kinds of *maya*: *yogamaya* and *mahamaya*. Mahamaya is an expansion of *yogamaya*, and both these mayas are different expressions of the Lord's internal potencies." (Srimad-Bhavatam 4.16.2 purport)

So, when we speak about our relationship with *maya*, in one sense we're speaking about two distinctly different relationships. One is with Krishna's illusory energy, which makes us forget Krishna, which causes suffering, and which we can be immersed in indefinitely in this material world. The other relationship is with Krishna's divine potency, in which we perceive Krishna's presence, mercy, and good will behind every happening and we relish and rejoice in that perception. In the poems that follow, the poets remark on both these aspects of *maya*—the delusive one that causes us to suffer the effects of time, as well as the divine one that draws us to Krishna's transcendent world.

From Krishna's point of view, *yogamaya* and *mahamaya* are both divine in that they both come from Him, and in that way they are one, much as the energy from a powerhouse is one. In our home, we may use that powerhouse energy for heating or cooling, as we like. Similarly, in our relationship with *maya* we also have a choice, as Krishna explains: "This divine energy of Mine, consisting of the three modes of material nature, is difficult to overcome. But those who have surrendered unto Me can easily cross beyond it." (*Bhagavad Gita* 7.14)

We can extricate ourselves from the dismal effects of *maya* (illusion) by dedicating ourselves to Krishna. Prabhupada explains, that to do this "one should (1) accept things favorable for discharging devotional service, (2) reject things unfavorable, (3) firmly believe that the Lord will always protect His devotee, (4) feel exclusively dependent on the mercy of the Lord, (5) have no interest separate from the interest of the Lord, and (6) always feel meek and humble." (*Teachings of Lord Chaitanya*, Preface)

These six items will transform our relationship with the suffering and frustration of *mahamaya* into the timeless, immeasurable joy of *yogamaya*, and some of the poets featured here express their yearning to do just that. What's more, even the process of dedication itself is accompanied by a relief from suffering and by joy as we progress from lust to love, from the coldness of unfruitful mundane relationships to the warmth of heartfelt relationships with Krishna and fellow Vaishnavas. The poets here also express the tests and hopes of this process.

Yet another meaning of *maya* is 'transcendental potency'. By the grace of this potency, we will know that nothing can exist without Krishna or for any purpose other than His pleasure. And knowing that, we will feel that potency within us. In Srila Prabhupada's words, "By the Grace of Krishna and the Spiritual Master, the dumb man can speak like a great orator, and a lame man can cross over a great mountain." (Letter to: Satsvarupa — Seattle 28 September, 1968) And sincere souls, we might add, can write deeply evocative and Bhakti-laden poetry.

The Search

Vrindavani Dasi

They say You were my dearest friend but
I cannot remember Your face.
They say it is more beautiful
than lotuses,
than shining moons,
than any metaphor.
I tear myself apart searching for memories of You
and find nothing but myself.
Where have You hidden Your lotus-like, moonlike face?

They say You are calling me but
I cannot remember Your voice.
They say it is more powerful
than thunder rumbling through the sky,
sweeter than a cuckoo's song,
so melodious it contains every note at once.
I strain my ears to hear You
—if it is true, shouldn't I hear You?—
and I hear nothing but the screaming of my mind.

They say You long to embrace me once more but
I cannot remember Your embrace.
They say Your arms are stronger than tree trunks,
Your shoulders like those of a lion,
Your skin softer than a fresh spring leaf.
I search frantically for Your embrace
—I am not stopping you!—
and I feel nothing but my own isolation.

They say you are always with me but
I cannot find you anywhere.

They say you are in my heart but
I think that I have none.

How long must I wait
Until you reveal yourself to me?

Here Today

Janavi Held

Here today   and yet
I am so far behind my time.

Perhaps I will be caught   in a torrent of unyielding mercy
perhaps I will drown there.

And yet I wonder if I should believe
in this momentary renunciation

perhaps it's born of fever
some virus   quickening my blood

forcing my mind to submit
to the impending death of skin   and all things frail.

Perhaps I should not believe
that my hands have let go of romance   and money

although   all who have come thus far
are a pale comparison.

It's so simple now
and so obvious:

I don't want to circle round
in these shape-shifting bodies

I want to be   as I am   always
never losing collected treasures

never lying to breathe
never killing to eat.

It seems such a simple request
and yet   I still lie here

planning what color to paint
my prison walls.

The Looney Bin of the Universe

Vrnda Devi Dasi

The flawed, the off-lawed live here
    uniformed in dying
by bars of time and space constrained
with bread-and-water love sustained
at universal cost maintained
    and universal crying.

In prison halls the rumor
    whispers of salvation
the Jailer comes Himself to plead
from cell to cell as if in need.
To save His friends He'd intercede—
    arrange their liberation.

Time off for good behavior.
    Could I be His friend?
Paroled and breathing once again
although I limp from ball-and-chain
and gratitude my only claim
    to meet Him at the end.

By Chance, a Chaunce

Niscala Dasi

By chance, a chaunce
Just jumped in my pot
There was no cook
For the curry we got.
The cook was invented
A long time ago
To explain the mysteries
That we now know.
Just another
Sad superstition
Like many another
Mad apparition!
By chance, a watch
Just came to be…
And here we are
Both you and me!
I can prove to you…
That my writing what's next
Are the laws of physics
Creating the text!
There's no intelligence
Behind my sweet rhyme
Left long enough, it
Can be caused by Time
It's true I deserve
No PhD
But my dear Dr. Hawking,
That's too true for thee!
If intelligence does not
With matter combine

To produce what we see
Then renounce your degree!
Physics produced it,
A child of chance
Thrust in the meaningless
Cosmic Dance...

Spring

Janavi Held

Nameless
My breath mixes with blue
And delirious summer diamonds
Those flowers

The heart of the earth
Bite into sunshine
Like the unfailing sting of rain
Warm color of mountains and wind

Warlike, always new
According to the almanac
Keeping track of ploughed lands
And vines

That keep moving to the sky
Up where pollen flies
And silence is victorious.
Ether, laden with the waves

Of twilight
Garlands the mortal chain
With endless impermanence.
Spring brings hope

Eyes watch
The forgotten dregs of winter
Following death
Where life takes her.

Flaming city of western sunset
Like hubris and tears
Darkens constellations
Of primitive aberrations

Of the exploding sounds
Of unspoken dawns
Growing from the anniversary
Of so many daybreaks

And the flesh of man falls
The ocean awaits his blood
At the edge of civilization
Reciting the testimony of flowers

Flower Arrows
Pranada Comtois

What happened
to the arrows of flowers
You were to send
into my heart?

I've long dreamt
of those arrows
hurled the cosmic distance
to scent inner chambers

my lifetime tendered
for onward travel
casts me
where I've never left
prison of my heart and mind

today I turn my
back against the wall
unscalable after all
slide down to rest

my pouch holds
nothing

have You abandoned
Your quiver for
another sport?

Masquerade

Tivra-bhakti Devi Dasi

Subtle and gross body
my garments
Again the upper clothes are lying on the floor,
and just the weightless nightgown is covering me
And again I will dress myself
into noblewoman's robe
with white silk and ruffles
or maybe a craftsman's
simple attire
According to destiny's design

Often looking for my new identity from my clothes
rather than inside

Repentance and Remorse
Urmila Devi Dasi

A gift was used as a weapon
Only causing pain
Therefore love could not deepen
Nor realization gain
One cannot go forward
While delighting in harm
Real mercy is thus covered
Open wound without a balm
So proud of kindness and mercy
Yet it's only a sham
If one's pleasure is dirty
And heart closed like a clam
Oh, Lord, an ocean of gratitude
To see the ugly truth
Of false beneficent beatitude
Twisted and uncouth
To long for the mirth and flowers
To ache for service and love
To want the joy of the bowers
Truth must open the bud

My Heart—Your Home
Promila Chitkara

The enemies
who vacated my heart
are lurking in the shadows
from the door left ajar.
O Supreme Enjoyer
when will you come
to grace the seat of my soul?
To protect me from the army
of anger, greed, and envy.
My feeble attempts
could only push them out
to the doorsill.
I hear the whispers of enemies—
their footsteps I hear.
louder and louder—
the walls of
my consciousness reverberate
the fear.
It must be my complacency
and forgetfulness of You—
the strongest weakness
that empowers even a lame foe.
Come home, my Lord.
Forgive my misgivings.
The sound of Your flute
will purify every inch
of the expanse of my being.
Come into my heart:
Your home.

Nigh High Travel
Pranada Comtois

If you cut human
from your heart
though you
triumphantly affix
a thousand angel wings
that softness stripped
cannot fly
to the soul's Beloved.

Tanke for Krishna

Promila Chitkara

On the soul's dark night
Where is the sound of the flute?
Oh lighten my heart
Blue God with peacock feather
Your 'lotus feet', my heaven

Ode to Mother Earth

Krsnanandini Devi Dasi

Contemplating your exhausted, semi-barren self,
    I cannot check the tears;
Contamination and exploitation, that's all
    you've known these last few years
Magnificent ones, obscure ones, have gloried in your splendor
Yet rare are those who reciprocate the services you render

Feeding, dressing, sheltering your offspring in every species of life;
In spite of your care, hatred, crime and pollution are rife.
    Bountiful, unlimited riches were invested in you
    To be shared by your posterity
    Now your resources are withdrawn
    And your Treasures are a rarity

Inevitably you now breathe a shallow breath
Respiration too deep could mean your death
How long can you drink of the poisonous waters
Apathetically offered by your sons and daughters

We know your Almighty Husband is the Creator Supreme
He is ready now, your health and wealth to redeem
    He has come in his wrath with the wind and the flood
    Not sharing, nor caring, we've shed unnecessary blood
Too late, we realize that by hurting the earth, we hurt too
And some few of us have decided to consider you
We're returning to simple, natural living
Hoping to correct our wrongs and be forgiven

Stay On

Sri Sundari Dasi

stay on, stay strong
at the end of this darkness, there is light

stay on, stay strong
in this chaos, there is divinity

Start to Run

Malini Jurelius

Will you let me know when it's time?
To leave and change again.
Will you whisper: "Just run, don't hide,
from the fears you call your own."

When time stops and moments start,
when you don't speak but start to talk.
When you live life, but life has just begun.
Start to run.

When you see the Light but it blinds you now.
Forget what's real to the rest of them.
Stop looking and see the world somehow,
where life for love, and love for life began.

Thank you for all the pain,
but I won't be back again.
Your traps are set on fire,
they will always be the same.
Please take me away from here,
this was never my home.

When time stops and moments start,
when you don't speak but start to talk.
When you live life but life has just begun.
Start to run.

The Sand Clock

Yasomati Devi Dasi

Just see how slowly life is running out,
The grains of sand in the sand clock just go by
Like peaceful, quiet, purplish whispers,
They never need to know your whereabouts,
They never ask you why.

Cold witnesses of our life and death
The seconds look at you and go,
But they will count your every single breath
And they will laugh at you as you will slowly grow,
Grow young and then grow old and die.

Life is an irony; we're born to surely die one day.
This is a place of death with death around us everywhere.
All that is left for us is to pray
And hope that He will hear our prayer.

Salvation for Dummies

Samapriya Devi Dasi

Riding around in a burnt out jalopy,
fuming and leaking it's all become sloppy
creaking and rattling tired and floppy,
maybe I should get a new shining copy.

Do I really want to go through all this again?
There are always problems from beginning to end.
Stand up for your rights your word to defend
and searching for someone on whom to depend.

We speak what we realize and it's become clear
most of us lonely and covered with fear.
The time now is coming, the last act to appear
when we reap what we sow and become what we hear.

Make our lives simple what more can we do?
It's passing us by as though time just flew.
But we have the answer the ultimate clue
on your knees to receive it, and it's given to you.

Handed to us through disciplic succession
in one strand of beads, the final concession.
We must take it up as our only possession.
Salvation for Dummies in this age of deception.

Demons of the Heart

Pooja Singh

Oh, how painful it is
to cut loose pieces of one's own heart
Feelings I have nurtured for ages
closely, deeply, confidentially.
Oh, the ill-feelings I have harbored,
The many unspoken thoughts,
Countless ulterior motives
And ill wishes for one and all.
In my mad rush for attention
How I have disregarded
Human decency, much less divinity
So I may rise, so I may shine.
I have gathered cheap accolades
From temporary admirers
And fed fuel to my enemies—
The demons of my heart.
Hankering for false tributes
Perhaps I even caught a glimpse of my foes
But I chose to turn away instead
And let my ego mask a heart's woes.
Oh, how painful it is
To live a life of pretense
To find shelter where none exists
To harbor demons within.

Ah, Yes
Vidya Devi Dasi

Is it a block
or is it a rock?
Is it a blessing in disguise?

How many are helping
in this game called life?
Forbidding us to live—
in strife;
More than we can bear!

Thank God, there are angels
who exist in the bubbles
of life's imagery.

Without them we might die;
Certainly fry!
In and out of shadows—
of happiness and distress.

Because it is all mercy:
Don't forget.

And the pain is merely attachment.

Dappled Winter Sunshine

Shyamasundari Dasi

Sitting here, under trees aged for centuries,
I feel my place in nature keenly,
I am here, but a moment,
And time will go on, as it did before,
These trees will see another girl sitting here,
admiring the play of light on their gnarled trunks,
They will hear the laughter,
cries and yells of another family,
The sun will warm the face of another,
Who might sit here
and wonder about the faces warmed long before hers,
Will she take a moment to capture the beauty around her?

Stop Cleansing the Cage

(A found poem from my guru's purport SB 1.2.8)
Visakha Dasi

Without knowing
the need
of the dormant soul,
one cannot be happy
simply
with emolument
of the body and mind.

Simply by cleansing the cage
of the bird,
one does not satisfy
the bird.
One must actually know
the needs of the bird himself.

The need
of the spirit soul
is that he wants to get out
of the limited sphere of
material bondage
and fulfill his desire
for complete freedom.
He wants to get out
of the covered walls
of the greater universe.
He wants to see
the free light
and the spirit.
That complete freedom
is achieved
when he meets the complete spirit,
the Personality of Godhead.

My Only Wish

Hladini Shakti Devi Dasi

I was in love. Remember that?
I couldn't sleep, I couldn't eat,
Your smile I couldn't forget.

Hearing Your voice and Your heart beat
my soul was singing, forcing me to dance
and I was laughing, laughing inside.

Feeling overwhelming happiness, joyful trance,
feeling Your presence, I'm choosing to hide,
hide from You, hide for eternity.

I'm choosing false pride.
I'm choosing insanity.
And I don't understand… Why?!
Why do I want to be alone?
How could I ever bid you goodbye?
Why did I leave our home…?
I don't know…
but please (again and again)
let my only wish be YOU.

This Poem Loves
Zoe Williams

This still, deep
Feeling in my chest.
This weight, weeps,
Cannot put to rest.

This love, feels,
Clouded and confused.
This closed, sealed,
Wounded and bruised.

This thought, repeats
Over in this mind.
This pattern, keeps
Me from God, I find.

This distance, far,
When really, it is close.
This sight, marred,
What do I love the most?

This drive, steers
To the endless ends.
This cost, near,
A price I can't defend.

This life, sold
Onto a maddened Earth.
This heart, molds
Into a fearful birth.

This soul, soiled
What is once, so pure.
This dirt, toiled
But there's a living cure.

This One, God
That connects us all.
This choice, given,
Causing us to fall.

This freedom, earned
When we look inside.
This heart, turned
To a loving guide.

This struggle, real,
To let go all we "know."
This surrender, kneel,
For God, we all bestow.

This love, His,
Cures all of dis-ease.
This life, This
God, how can we please?

The Other Dream

Champak Manjari Dasi

Spirals. Musical notes.
Hands that play keys,
and hearts. The moon
calls us out to play,
but don't dream when you rise.

Or, dream, but don't remain
in that dream, for it will end.
Who will you complain to then?
Everything invites us to dream!

There are illusionary dreams
that entangle me with this world.
And there is a real dream
that drives me toward You.

I long to dream that dream!
The other dream.
Krishna! Don't forget
to dream about me too.

CHAPTER SIX

PRAYERS

"O Lord of Madhu
as the Ganges flows to the sea without hindrance,
let my attention be constantly drawn to You
without being diverted to anyone else."

Queen Kunti (Bhagavat Purana, Canto 1.8.42)

A Conversation with God
Janavi Held

The rising, the softly reaching of the heart towards the Divine: What is this impulse to reach into what is unseen and give all attention to this single act of prayer? What is it that we are searching for? In my life, prayer began with one single question: why am I here? This question arising from my heart appeared like a homing beacon and the first four words of a conversation.

Through prayer we can uncover our longing for communion with the Supreme Divine, as the act of prayer becomes a conversation or a perpetual meditation on that relationship; as such, prayer is both the question and the answer.

As the years pass, I find that this conversation grows both murky and vivid in turns. My heart reaches out in times of trouble stretching towards God for comfort and answers to the secrets of living and dying; for knowledge and understanding, for divine love to wrap around me and fill the empty places with the gift of transcendental love.

During times of ease, my prayers may speak of gratitude, and yet I still strive to collect the words pouring from my heart into an offering to the Lord. I do so in the hopes that despite the ups and downs I may encounter I will remain connected to this conversation and not become too distracted by the busy world from this important relationship.

My actions in this world can be transformed into prayers; a prayer of appreciation springs from my heart as I commune with nature, with the precious things that God has made, and as a poet I find that the chattering mind must step aside to say a prayer asking for assistance from the Supreme Creator. And so I see prayer and poetry as returning the elements to the elemental; like a child collecting flowers from her mother's garden and bringing them to her as a gift.

My Lord,
these words
you give me
I arrange
like a bouquet
of tender flowers
bringing
them to You
secretly
hoping
to make
You
smile
and
if You should smile
at me
I will run
and collect baskets
and baskets
of words
to lay at Your
sweet feet.

    Poetry and prayer have been intertwined since the earliest recorded poems. Within the ancient Rig Veda, brought forward from antiquity via oral recitation, we find esoteric verse contemplating the origins of creation.

    Poetry appears as prayer in the ancient culture of the Sumerian carved on stone tablets by the moon Priestess, Enheduanna, born in 2300 B.C. At times, prayer is simply a joyful celebration of the heart's reunion with God; as the Sufis spin and write their beautiful love poems, as the Bhakti Yogi dances and chants the Lord's many names. We find poetic prayers by women among the Christian mystics, such as St. Teresa of Avila (c. 1515-15582) who wrote, "I found completeness/ When each breath began to silently say the name/of my Lord..." And Jews living life by the Kabala weave their lives and hearts into an offering of words, and dance, and song; all drawing nearer to their Beloved, as Rabia of Basara, the Sufi saint (c. 717-801) wrote, "Show me where it hurts, God said, and every cell in my body burst into tears before His tender eyes."

I find that within the Bhakti tradition prayer is the heart rising to reach for that affectionate Supreme Soul who truly loves us and wants to begin a conversation with us as soon as we decide that, "Love is all you need," and that the fleeting pleasures of this temporary life will no longer hold our hearts as much as we desire to hold to that Supreme Personality. A great saint in the Bhakti tradition, Queen Kunti, prayed, "I wish that all those calamities would happen again and again so that we could see You again and again, for seeing You means that we will no longer see repeated births and deaths." (Śrīmad-Bhāgavatam 1.8.25)

Queen Kunti's prayers follow in the wake of seemingly endless tragedies, including the death of her husband and repeated threats against the lives of her five sons. Yet her prayers indicate that her main concern is her relationship with God and returning to Him—no longer rotating from one life to another in this world of the temporary. As she continues her prayers, her longing for the presence of God, and her love for Him, are expressed, "O Gadādhara [Krishna], our kingdom is now being marked by the impressions of Your feet, and therefore it appears beautiful. But when You leave, it will no longer be so." (Śrīmad-Bhāgavatam 1.8.39) Towards the end of her prayers—comprised of twenty-six verses—she expresses her desire to have her heart and consciousness exclusively focused on Him. "O Lord of Madhu, as the Ganges forever flows to the sea without hindrance, let my attraction be constantly drawn unto You, without being diverted to anyone else." (Śrīmad-Bhāgavatam 1.8.42)

In this chapter we discover women following in the ancient tradition of the Bhakti Yogini, flinging their hearts to God and requesting to be held tight in His embrace as they walk through life discovering their own personal relationships with all that is eternal. As they maneuver through this world via this inner dialogue with their most ancient Friend.

In this world of temporary treasures, heartbreaking tragedies—this place where monuments are built to dissolving histories—it is good to know that within our hearts there resides our primeval friend who is happy to listen to our cares and concerns, and who understands our heart's truest desire even better than we do, and who is guiding us home to Him on this vehicle of prayer; this divine act of speaking and listening.

Thoughts on Prayer

Nanda Carlson

The act of prayer
not for something I want,
desire, or desperately need
but to pray in awe
of a vastness,
incomprehensible
a true mystery
where I am held, tenderly
part of an expansive
eternal wholeness.
So big, beyond the edges
and borders
there is freedom within
a Love beyond reason.
Even in this tiniest of moments,
it is made known,
it is there, as it always was
Source, the Divine, Reality, Truth…
always present, never alone, never waiting.
So I pray
from this experience
with humility and gratitude
for being a part of this
Great Love,
in relationship with the Divine
and all others
from this knowing comes
a way of living in this world.
We are love, we are loved,
we act from love,

our perception, choices,
words and thoughts
begin to change and unfold
from a place much bigger
than who we think we are.
As Love moves through us
we pray in gratitude,
we pray to remember,
we pray for love
and for that eternal connection
and all that we do and are
becomes Devotion.

Incense

Gopalpreet Taya Malakian

The air is thick
with the incense of our prayers.
Each stick lit with an intention,
a call,
a vibration,
sent out from the heart
to the Universe,
and back again.
The fragrance of spices, herbs, blossoms and woods,
gathered from far reaches,
ground together by hand with prayers recited over them.
Each stage,
its own blessing.
Here
I add my stick of incense
to the altar
and send my hearts prayer
across the Universe and back.

Mandir

Braja Sorensen

"If these walls could speak…." but they do;
Words uttered through eternity
Whispering beauty softly spoke
Poetry in stone.

What wisdom, sunk into these walls?
"Lean closer," they say. "We will tell
of sages old, mantras chanted,"
Poetry in song.

What tales in smoke of frankincense?
Exotic, the perfume of time
perspires from pores of ancient stone
Poetry in scent.

Humble presence, the marble floor
Worn soft and smooth by the faithful
Slow forging of paths trod with love
Poetry in motion.

Rapturous notes, song of the heart
Echoing through the centuries
Continual cycle of words
Poetry in devotion.

Timeless elements combine, an
eternal poetic embrace
All for the pleasure of the Lord;
Poetry of love.

"If these walls could speak," and they do—
of eternal devotion, prayer,
timeless acts of love
Poetry of eternity.

Temple of the Heart

Krsnaa Mary Devi Dasi Fitch

What is a place
that is holy?
Where does sacredness reside?
How can a heart cease to be phony
And finally see what's inside?
The doors are golden and heavy
They creek from lack of use
This temple is tiny, one of many
but within, there resides the truth
A chamber of Love
Filled with Sacred Sound
and depth beyond our wildest dreams
so simple it seems
but such a rare occasion
to look inside the heart
and feel a revelation
that Love
That beauty
And warm golden softness
that allay all our fears
Comes from our constant companion
A Friend who is infinitely dear
He holds our hand
as we face the world
and try to find our place
among the garbage and the grace
Our heart, our temple
A sanctuary that is there
whenever we need it
no need to buy a ticket
only our desire, and trust
of our self is needed to open that heavy gate.

Offering My Heart

Kruti Patel

Giving my heart to another can be a painful experience.
They may not reciprocate my feelings;
They may cause me heartache and pain;
They may leave me feeling lost and alone.
But you, Krishna, you're always there for me.
Silently and sweetly waiting for me to turn to you.
Waiting for the moment that I realize it's you that I love most dearly.
Today, I make a promise to offer my heart to you.
In my offering, I pray you keep my heart safe and sheltered
I pray you keep me always at your lotus feet
But most of all, I pray you never let me go.

Listen
Krsnaa Mary Devi Dasi Fitch

Casting a gaze across the hazy river
To a star above the twinkling lights
I hold the stone, feel the breeze and quiver
And start to throw a wish up to the heights

Let me be above this world
Let me know more than I see
Let my heart become unfurled
So that God will hear my plea

I pray like this night after night
Standing in the dark, looking into the light
But never does my soul connect
Nor do I gain what I expect

Till one day under my hands I see
A leaf connected to a tree
And to that tree springs earth and ground
And so I see an answer is found

Whilst I've been cooing up towards the sky
Striving for what is beyond my reach
The answer I seek the ground will supply
The Mother, answers to me She will teach

I am of grass and of hills and of dirt
Within me God is alive and alert
He speaks, only I have to listen
Then my true self He will christen

Knowledge, Eternity and Bliss
Make up the dance of consciousness
Inside my earthly womanly form
Brews a vast unyielding storm

A hunger to know, and to love and to live
And to listen, hear, absorb and give
The secret that life is no boring task
But a chance for us to look inside and ask

What we are, where we've been and are going
Why is it we keep ourselves from growing
Past the thicket, and over the hedge
Round the bend and into the edge

Of the boxes and caves we create
Full of racism, prejudice and hate
Breaking free and coming to find
That the trick was coveting the blind

Thinking they had the answer to give us
When we knew it all along

May I Still You...

Indu Arora

Still as I am
Energy moves through me
Waves and thrill
Thrills and chills
Within I move
Outside... still
May it invoke the still in you
As I still myself, May I still you!

Do Not Wait to Pray

Gopalpreet Taya Malakian

Do not wait to Pray.
Let each breath be your prayer.
Do not wait until you are in a sacred space to pray.
Pray in the streets filled with traffic and noise
Pray in the middle of the mundane where it is least expected.
Do not wait until your hair is past your shoulders
or shaved entirely away.
Pray in the moment you wake up.
Pray just before you enter sleep
and every second in between.
When you don't know what to do—pray.
In your moments of great clarity and conviction—pray.
Let each movement become your prayer,
each gesture divine.
Let every cell in your body sing the same prayer—
vibrating in the most reverent song.
Let the lines blur so that prayer becomes not just
something you do,
but the state of being in which you live,
in which you love
in which you pray.

Drunk

Jhilmil Breckenridge

I'm drunk on spring,
the newness of shoots sprouting,
birds chirping in joyful cacophony.

I'm drunk on morning,
the eagle that perches, preening,
dusty skies touched with vermilion.

I'm drunk on morning prayer,
bells in a faraway temple chiming,
while the muezzin calls the faithful.

I'm drunk on life,
every breath a gift, every movement a prayer,
may I stay drunk forever!

Devotee Devotee, Krishna's Calling You

Krsnanandini Devi Dasi

Devotee, devotee, Krishna's calling you
There's something He wants you and me to do
    Call His name, talk of His fame
    Share with people His loving aim

Love and serve Krishna—no other reason to be
For all the living things are parts of Him, you see?
    If we all remember Krishna and talk of Him
    Our lives grow—in and out—like a tree stem

So devotee, devotee, you pray for me and I for you
That we will always do what Krishna wants us to!

Prayer to Conquer the Mind
Kaivalya Sundari Devi Dasi

My mind is battling my soul:
Is Krishna Consciousness the goal?
In the waves of duality I toss and turn,
Is it Love of God for which I yearn?
Spiritual dreams and material schemes:
Are the two compatible themes?
Why do I search for happiness
in the strangle of Maya's caress?
In the struggle to be good
am I doing what I should?
Please give me strength to tame my mind
and leave countless desires behind.
I know not a day goes by
that I do not ask the question: *"Why?"*
Please let me have the eyes to see
that you are always here with me!

Tears

Krishna Rose

The waters of purity
From behind the mask
Times bitter flood doth rise
Our beauty
May perish
And be lost
For all time
For all but our eyes

When winds have gathered
And sun and moon burned dim
The things we lost are gone
In the reflection
Our souls glisten
For a moment
When a prayer is murmured
With wistful yearning
Adoring
For in truth
It is in Your realm
I long to breathe

The One True Goal

Radha Mulder

Oh Lord of Creation,
Maintainer of All,

Oh Master of Universes,
of Galaxies infinite,
yet small,

Oh Lord of the heart,
Oh Compassionate and Kind,

You've brought me to You,
yet still I remain blind.

However difficult the path may seem,
I now know life is merely a dream.

A long procession of desires and fears,
life after life of hopes and tears.

The duality,
the struggle,
the longing of the soul,

In the end of it all,
You are the only
One true goal.

Petals of Grace

Debra Sue Lynn

Lord, I come to You this night
offering a humble prayer of gratitude...

Creator of all the worlds!
Cause of all causes!
For Your glory, Lord, hear this
heart's song:

You are my Rock, my Fortress. Guarded.
Protected. Sheltered, but not hidden.
You are the Changeless Now, the Absolute Truth.

It doesn't matter how difficult the journey seems,
how exposed the heart must be;
for until You come to the doorstep of one's heart,
knocking, waiting, breaking down all walls of resistance,
melting all obstacles to peace,
we circle,
suffering endlessly while we wait, wait for...
redemption, redemption that never seems to come.

When our hearts, our minds surrender,
beckon and, bid You stay, then Lord, in receptive silence
    You arise.

When the seeds of Faith germinate
into racemes of Friendship, then on the stem of patience
Your petals of grace embrace me.
You awaken all my centers
releasing Eternal Springs of Bliss within this soul.
Though love resides within, peace must be earned.

When no one and nothing comforts me,
Only Your Word, written upon ancient scrolls,
bold texts of Sacred Scripture unfold to grant me peace.

You, Supreme Benefactor, Source of all that IS,
only Your mellifluous song stills this restless heart.

You are Love's celestial rhapsody,
the longest and the shortest step,
the most narrow and straight way to freedom.

Your pure essence,
Your ineffable Spirit resides at the core,
in the fiber of my soul's eternal quest.

With unquenchable thirst, unsatisfied hunger,
I come, surrendered,
kneeling at Your feet to the Altar of Holy Silence,
in Absolute knowing.

Holding fast to Your Word,
and in Your Name, I proclaim:
This Journey, this Quest WILL... IS
leading me on the only, true, Pathway Home.

Sigh

Mahalaksmi Devi Dasi

Invisible, impalpable, it can never be seen by strangers
Nor has had ever a mailer and goes beyond containers
Sigh extols, raising beyond boundaries all bold emitters
Whilst those evoking it so, strengths, enriches and inspires
Sigh is manna descending from the divine abode on lovers
Nourishment meant to satisfy our beloved unflinching adviser
Sigh sustains thirsty souls hankering for real love, true believers
Liberating sigh lightens cold, freezing, hard, tight, dark
    iron fetters
Sigh is love without expecting any reward, nor even
    sweetest of manners
Most sacred of all actions an offering from the temple,
    which is deeply inner
Unceasingly flowing towards your commanding feet, for
    you to bestow the diffuser
A matching destiny that shall bring sense to this hankering
    soul, which is meant to be yours

I Surrender Unto You

Navakishori Devi Dasi

Deserted, abandoned, cast off,
caught unaware
shocked, lonely and hurt
over and over again

Millions of lifetimes
of finding Gajendra within myself.
How many experiences
before I follow Gajendra?

Futility of false shelters,
belief in false promises
Why that pull towards falsity?
When You are the Absolute Truth!

Your loving embrace,
Your ocean of compassion,
Your glance, Your love, Your patience
should draw me in

You are the controller
You are Achyuta
You have kept Your promise at all times
You are bhakta-vatsala

Hey Govinda!
I surrender unto You,
I surrender unto You,
I, finally, surrender unto You.

Do You Believe Me Yet?

Jagattarini Dasi

Will You be there for me at the end?
Visible, beyond golden effulgence?
"We don't touch the real problems of life"
Someone wise is speaking.

I dreamt I cried seeing You in a temple
There is hope but so many doubts.
Like an ostrich I waste so much time
My head in a realm providing no shelter.

There is blue in the sky because You are blue
Look up again. Reflect. Can you see?
Try. Travel trying. Travel to try and see.
Because the end becomes the next beginning.

You say "I shall release you."
"There is no difficulty loving Me."
No problems but so many problems
Will you take care of me until I learn to love?

Tender pink lotus petals unfurl in a reply
"Serve me as you now serve yourself.
Expect trouble here. Maya is very strong.
So carry on safely towards reality and home."

Sayana Arati

Anuradha Sakhi Devi Dasi

When my time here is through...
Dear mind
be so kind
as to take me to
the place
where hearts
echo with the beat of a drum
eyes entrance
each song enchants us
till we're
lost
happily in the web of His love
thoughts of self-preservation
defeated by sweet liberation
of the soul
which sings
swaying
in Gokula's candle lit kingdom

My Heart Sings

Ananda Rupa Devi Dasi

Praying to you:
  A cry, or a smile.
I forget to breathe
  once in a while.

Sweet incense and flowers
  when the bell rings
And just like that
  my heart sings!

CHAPTER SEVEN

SEVA

I am in love with the service I got today,
with saints around who blew pains away.
Higher and higher I want to fly
holding up hands, prayers reaching the sky:
"My Lord, engage me in Your service!"
…My heart has two open wings now!

Mohini Madhavi Devi Dasi

Service is my Constant Companion

Braja Sorensen

Service, or *seva*, is not an alien concept to most. In any well-bred atmosphere of home, we can find the principle of service instilled in the young minds being brought up in such environments; we see it extend into a part of one's nature, sometimes to such a degree that their lives become simply one of service, or *seva*. Spiritually, we see young women renouncing marriage and children and entering convents; monks entering ashrams; ministers, *pujaris* (priests), and all manner of spiritual institute lifers or congregational members: all of them dedicating their lives to service to God and His people. Materially, we see young men and women offering their lives in service to humankind: in fire departments, hospitals, paramedic services, armed forces, the Navy, and so on.

For many, service is ingrained so deeply there can be nothing else. In the Bhakti yoga tradition, however, that service is directed towards the object of one's affection and aspiration: Radha and Krishna, and even more so, *seva* is offered to Their associates and intimate friends.

In the *Bhagavad Gita* it is said, "No living entity is exempt from rendering service to other living beings, and therefore we can safely conclude that service, *seva*, is the constant companion of all, and that the rendering of service is actually the eternal religion of every living being."

In Sanskrit this "eternal religion" is known as *sanatana-dharma*. But it is not "religion" in the way one might normally think of religion. Although one might change their "religion," the inherent principle of *seva* exists in every living being. That is *sanatana-dharma*. And what a wonderful chapter to read, and view through the lens of eternal knowledge from the Gita! For the spiritualist, there are daily spiritual practices that override the dominant material nature. But the Gita also says, without developing an attachment to *seva*, one can never hope to be free of the binding forces of the material energy.

I cannot separate myself from this concept of *seva* any more than I can separate myself from my name, because the word "seva" is, indeed a part of my name: Braja Sevaki Dasi. This name was given to me over twenty years ago during a ceremony held in honor of my having entered into the Vaishnava *diksha* process, in which one formally accepts a spiritual master, makes vows and is given a spiritual name. My name means "one who serves (*dasi*) the female servants, or damsels (*sevaki*) of Vrindavan (*braja*), which is the home of Radha and Krishna. The damsels are the *gopis*, or Radha's friends who serve her. So my name means that I am the servant of the servants of Radha, and I cherish every aspect of the name.

Nor can I separate my name from my work as a writer. For I write to serve, to give— even to one person—an answer they're seeking, a meaning they've looked for, a moment they've waited for. It can be just one word. It doesn't mean I have to write masterpieces, it just means I attempt to serve others through the words that I write. Seva is thus never offered in the expectation of receiving profit, or fame, or of satisfying any other external demand. It is meant, instead, to become one's *sanatana-dharma*, as I feel writing has become to me: my constant companion.

What better mood, then, with which to enter into this chapter, embracing the consciousness that all we read in the following pages can take us deeper into our eternal religion, *seva*, and far from the ever-present modes of material nature.

Learning to Love

Vrnda Priya Devi Dasi

Love is not unconditional unless tested
And aren't you the one who has claimed to love?
Go! Ask your Creator: "Why me? This is wrong!"
But understand that faith means
Holding fast to this freezing branch
Even when the leaves are long gone

Soothe the Suffering of Your Heart

Sumati Govinda

Unconditional love: an infinitely flowing river from source
    back to source
Healing, purifying, nurturing, and supporting
Thankfulness is not enough
Gratitude is not enough
Humble prostrations are not enough
Embody love
The highest praise, the greatest gift, the needed offering
Soothe the suffering of creation with an infinite waterfall of love.

The Hand Broom's Grip

Pranada Comtois

A plastic sheath at the top
  clamps stems' extended spikelets
    a simple wand of soft, brown grass—
      tail of coarse feathers—

sweeps slate, tile, dirt, marble floors
  dusts rails, walls, screens, balconies, doors
    held by the frail-thin bent at waist
      left hand's backside rests on lower spine

shaft in right hand
  coaxes grass-tuft to tickle the floor—
    classic pose seen all over India
      seems rooted in the ancient: this is the only way.

In the old man's hand at his back
  a small square shard of rusted metal
    serves as dust pan for the piles
      of red rose petals, white flowers, dirt

from the insistent stream
  of pilgrims' bare feet shuffling
    the hand broom leaves nothing:
      its tiny grassy fingers grab

remnants of lives—
  looking on, she says
    let me foster such humility, simplicity
      then closes her eyes.

Without sound spacious floor swept
  in three easy minutes
    guided between chanters, pacing and sitting
     in the white marble temple

this the sweepers are allowed,
  one generation to the next:
   brush, brush, brush
    with the brown grass broom.

GRAFFITI

Bhakti Lata Dasi

I walk past the gutters
littered with trash
and the walls scrawled
with shapeless letters.
Music with no melody,
only beats and mutters,
blares from speakers.
Lined, unsmiling faces
and crossed arms
greet me on the platform.
The train arrives with
a blast and the rhythmic
ga-gumph,
ga-guuumph,
ga-guuuuuuumph…
The doors open with a hiss.
The floor rumbles beneath me,
we pass building
after building
scarified with
more
and more graffiti
that all looks the
same same same.
Graffiti scratches surround me
on the window and seat,
on the walls.
A man across the aisle
misses his stop, curses loudly.

I arrive at the Bhakti Center for a festival
drained
by the City.
Drained by the way
We
and I
graffiti our lives
with chitter and chatter
and curses.

I'm on the schedule to
sing kirtan in 15 minutes.
I heave a sigh and
head to the temple room.
I am washed with the scent
of incense and
the holy name.
I thought that I had needed
to sleep
but after a half an hour
of singing
I just want to stay here
right here
in front of God
for the next seven days
and graffiti my heart
with the holy name.

Tearing Out a Bit of My Heart

Mitravinda Devi Dasi

I tear out the pictures of the very large and beautiful first
volume of Srimad Bhagavatam,
Or are these bits of my heart?
A gift from their Guru, to be shared— hand to hand,
copied and copied again
from those copies by an unending number of thirsty,
suffering souls.

Beyond the Finish border, train grinds to a screaming halt.
My compartment fills with border guards. Russian talk,
passport, luggage, I show and nod.

I have long prepared for this. Spiritual contraband carefully
disguised:
Any of it could buy me a one-way ticket to Siberia!
Will he detect my nerves? My heart is racing to Krishna,
who calmly takes my breath
and soul into perfect peace. I'm shielded.

Cold stare, scanning me for fear: gaze slowly falling
down to window ledge, Srimad Bhagavatam resting there
casually: too big to hide. As if in a dream I see my hand
pick it up, open it, and show the English and Sanskrit, now
appreciating my orders to remove all the pictures.

Not understanding a word, it was now up to him. Split
second, Supersoul hints: "Get on with your day." He turned
on his heel, and was gone.

First part of my mission completed!
I passed the rest of the train ride in great joy, blessed with
the oblivion of what was coming.
Still, all is Krishna's mercy!

The Beating of My Heart
Devesani Radhika Dasi

Before I met you, I was shadowed in darkness
Covered in ignorance with a passion unfound.
My life had excitement, but it didn't last
Looking for love, I searched all around.

I knew you from a distance, not enough to tell
I knew people loved you; you put them under spell.
What would you do to me if I got near?
I decided to get closer, rejecting all fear.

I was determined to know you, though you caused me much pain.
And working daily with you, my energy would drain.
But I realized without you, would make me insane.
I became addicted to you; you were my cocaine.

You've always been there when the going gets tough.
With your attractive mood, I can't get enough.
You are patient and calm when I make a mistake.
You are in my thoughts from the moment I wake.

Our bond has now grown to much more than before.
Whenever I see you, I crave for you more.
I've found my passion that's in my heart's core.
You are the awesome mridanga that sits on the floor.

Kitchen Prayer to Lord Nityananda

Madhava Lata Devi Dasi

Lord Nityananda Balaram,
presiding Deity of objects of seva
Lord of remembrance and wakefulness,
let chintamani touch this place,
this fire, these utensils
and the gunas remain at the doorway.
Let sugar, salt, flour
become syllables of mantras
and to my mind
every flavour be sound
unrelated to the palate.
Let Bhakti Devi be the Ishvari
of my limbs, eyes and actions
and along with this fire,
like one in the dwellings of Vraja,
be compelling attraction and pleasure
for the Wonderful Thief,
so might come and sample from the pots.
Let whatever results
be worthy to host
Your saliva
Deliverer of conditioned souls.

Once Remembered
Madhavi Lata Dasi

All I know I think
I want to see your
Light bright darkness
Holding forever in
Your endless gazing eyes
Loving me unconditionally
While I always forget you,
Once remembered forgetting
Now longing for another glimpse
Rainbow stream carves love
Into my covered heart
Shearing the veil
Whispers eternally foretell
Flowing into that secret
Flute-singing divine
Connection

The Heart's Beat

Gopalpreet Taya Malakian

There is a beating in my heart
that matches the stepping of my feet,
that is in time with the sound of the drums,
which patterns the rhythm of the Universe.
When I return to this pulsing inside of me
I instantly unite with all the songs of the spheres
and I am at peace.
From this peace I can play with the rhythm,
contributing my voice,
my song,
to the orchestra of this Universe.
Uniting my entire being,
in harmony,
with this entire Being.

Nights of Kartika

Shyama Bhakti Devi Dasi

The sun sets
welcoming the month of Kartik,
sprinkles of pink
stud the most bluish sky
recalling the palms of Your hands…
so delicate, so reassuring.
This nightfall of gentle breezes
scented of juniper,
inspires me, within.
This most magical month
of small lamps—
their aroma of melting butter
warming the devoted hearts,
cause soulful melodies to resound
and my thoughts, as if winged,
fly elsewhere,
somewhere.
There, amidst green woods,
with the sound of Your small reed flute
You make Your eternal playmates
dance
intoxicated by eternal Love.

Heart of a Vaishnavi

Seva-mayi Dasi

I served you at Your temple today,
sorting through flowers, discarding that which
was unacceptable so only the best could be
offered at Your altar.
Oh Govinda, in much the same way I pray You.
Sort out the desires of my heart,
so that that which remains is only that which
is most pleasing to You.
I pray that you give me the heart of a vaishnavi,
When I feel sorrow, may it only be my heart's
angst at feeling separation from You, dear Lord.
When I feel joy, may it be the joy that rises
up from within at being immersed in Your Names.
When I feel attraction, may it be the attraction
that draws my heart and mind deep into the
remembrance of Your many pastimes and qualities.
When I feel distressed, may it be because I can't
get enough of Your sweetness.

Like a bee hovering from flower to flower
may I never cease my pursuit of You,
my anxious restlessness driving me ever onwards.
The world shifts and changes with each passing moment.
But Your love is eternal, and remains ever fixed,
weaving existence together.
May all glories be to You—
Creator, Destroyer, and Divine Lover.

How Can I Be of Service?

Kelly Noyes

Words cannot express what I feel:
something so new and so real

You were far away and yet now so close
you reach into my heart and find the right note

Pressing it gently; the music I hear
listening with delight I smile from ear to ear

You are here and all around
I was lost and once again found

You come through with grace
there you are once more to replace

the energy and the love that was lost
to show me that I am not so much the boss

You reel me back in through rivers and the night sky
you cast a hue of blue where I lie

Speaking ever so gently I know it is you
please help me to know how I can be of service to *you.*

To the Source

Urmila Devi Dasi

You are the source of all sweet smells
Yet we offer perfume-laden oil

You are the softest most delicate beauty
Yet we massage your mildest form

You are the source of all enjoyment
Yet we seek to serve Your senses

You want the happiness of the jivas
Yet we serve to give you happiness

Loving Kiss

Jen Walls

Gift Krishna your all
make steps—no matter how small;
wake sunshine's bliss-bloom

Lift breaths of beauty
speak with care—inside-prayer;
spark kindness alive

Fly with Madhava
spray light-joy—Radha flowers;
glow supreme moment

Meditate heart's peace
pray bright fields—cosmic fountains;
flow Love-Consciousness

Share soul's worthiness
bless divine heart—restrain mind;
extend loving kiss

I Am in Love

Mohini Madhavi Devi Dasi

I am in love with the service I got today,
with saints around who blew pains away.
In love with early mornings, the loud sound of a conch shell.
I am in love with the first Darshan,
I am in love with the smile of a bluish God!
In love with the compassion of His Beloved
With His three bending Form: curly hair, beautiful eyes!
Oh I am in love with the life I am living these days
In love with the sound of a *mridanga* and *karatal*
tik taka taka tak played for the pleasure of the Lord:
A sound that moves me to join my palms in pranam to parampara.
I am in love with singing *'Vande Guroh shri charanaravindam!'*
And the Maha Mantra: Hare Krishna Hare Krishna…
I am in love with that cry but do not know the reason why.
In love with the well wishes I have for all:
"May your futures be happy and bright!"
Oh I am in love with my owning no one,
what to speak of my own life!
I am in love with giving up material wishes
Oh how free I feel when I make such decisions!
No matter what happiness and distress will come
let me not spend my life trapped by either one.
But rather, getting ready to go back Home!
I am in love with dancing:
Higher and higher I want to fly
holding up my hands, with prayers that reach the sky:
"My Lord, engage me in Your service!"
I am in love! My heart has two open wings now!
Hare Krishna! How sweet life is when one is in love!!!

Spinning in Love
Malvika Unnithan

Spinning around from here to there,
not really knowing where:
Holding on to someone dear—
My Love.

Spinning around, going with the flow,
from the heart, not just for show:
Holding on to something dear—
His Love.

Spinning around, dancing in trance,
hoping someday I'll receive his glance:
Holding on to all we have—
Our Love.

CHAPTER EIGHT

DIVINE NATURE

*"Tree heavy with fruit
Knowing strength comes from its roots
Bows with gratitude"*

Jai Gaurangi Devi Dasi

Divine Nature
Rukmini Walker

Seeing God in Nature, and Nature in God, is intrinsic to Bhakti. In the *Bhagavad Gita*, the Supreme Divinity, as Krishna, says: "I am the taste of water... I am the light of the Sun and the Moon... I am the original fragrance of the earth..." (BG 7.8, 9) Each morning, before rising, I pray to Mother Earth:

> "O Mother Earth, I offer my humble obeisance unto you, who are the wife of Lord Vishnu and the residence of the oceans, and who is decorated with so many mountains. Please forgive me for stepping on you."

This offering of respect to Mother Nature is foundational to cultivating a spiritual practice. In the Bhakti tradition, the natural world around us is seen as a shadow, or reflection, of another world—divine in nature—which is eternal and vibrant with joy and knowledge. There, everything exists only for the sake of reciprocating love with the Beloved Lord. When the natural beauty in this world, serves to inform us of the beautiful nature of the divine world, it participates in this divine love.

Lord Krishna explains in the *Bhagavad Gita* that Nature is divine, belongs to Him, and is very difficult to understand. This is because Mother Nature is full of paradox: both in what we see and what remains unseen. Her many faces—which change from moment to moment—can bewilder us in her complexity. While Mother Nature's beauty and peace inspire us, her power to unleash devastation in the flash of a moment has the power to terrify us. Yet Krishna says that one who seeks His shelter, in devotion, can easily cross beyond the delusions of this shadowy realm (BG 7.14).

At night, in spring, I hear bullfrogs croaking in the pond behind our house. Who is the little bullfrog crying for in such a loud voice? Some might be irritated by the noise. One in love might say he cries for his beloved. One who is aware of the temporal nature of this world might say he is calling his own death to come in the form of a snake. For another, the sounds of bullfrogs might bring to mind sacred passages from ancient Bhakti texts that describe Krishna playing with his cowherd boyfriends in the forest of Vraja, imitating frog-jumps as they play. Therefore, the relationship nature plays in our life depends very much on our perspective.

The Bhakti perspective is about love. When we desire to turn toward Krishna and approach Him in love, He, dwelling in our hearts, gives us the understanding by which our darkness is destroyed and our perspectives illuminated (BG 10. 10-11). In awakening our loving relationship with the Divine, Mother Nature reveals aspects of the divine to us.

As such, she becomes our Supreme Mother, called Hara. She extends her grace to help us achieve the grace of the Supreme Father, Hari, or Krishna: the seed-giving Father and origin of all existence (BG 9.17). When Mother Nature becomes aware that we are honoring and respecting her, as God's beloved, she blesses the world with divine grace, peace and bounty.

The poems collected in this chapter are the voices of women who, in the quiet of their introspection, are observing Nature in connection, in harmony, with her Source, her Beloved, the Origin of us all. Their words transform the familiar, the everyday and the ordinary aspects of nature—such as rain, snow, wind, a tiny seed, a flower—into participants in helping us taste the eternal. Drink deeply of their wisdom, of their conscious, observant gratefulness. This is a place where, for a few precious moments, the curtain of Material Nature is lifted by grace; where we catch a glimpse of Divine Nature—which is joyful, radiant and alive— and allow the beauty of the natural world around us to awaken our love of God.

The Loud Quiet of Snow

Ananda Vrindavan Devi

It is the gift of snow
the quietness it brings
the inch by inch build up
of small things making big
the loud quiet of snow
we can hear the stillness
the muffled sounds
of the world
so loudly absent
it gives us a taste
of the great quietness
that lives within us
brought to life
by each Name chanted
falling softly into
the depths of our very own selves
to clear the way for us to
hear the sounds of
another place, another world
the great quietness of
the place we left behind
so long ago.

Watching Snow from an Upstairs Window

Rukmini Walker

Grace
Could come sideways
Flying, drifting up
Or falling down…

In microscopic symmetry
Each way unique
Or flaky clumps
Pouring down
On the brown parched heart.

Or, as a web of lace
Circling round me
Holding me from falling
Cradling me, in branches of tall trees.

White etched trees reach upward
Catching grace
In infinite outstretched fingers
Roots go deep
To drink the mystery
To taste the eternal.

I am held in *sanga*
Reaching back generations
Their arms upraised, hearts uplifted
Reaching up, pouring down,
Flying all around.

My Winter's Prayer

Nanda Carlson

There lies a seed within,
deep inside one's heart,
resting in the womb of the Divine Mother.
This wintertime of hibernation is a holding place
always there, protecting, waiting
for the Springtime of life.

When the seed begins to open
to the Sun within,
we remember His Light and Love.

Nourishing, caring
for this tiny seed,
this sweet delightful bud,
the flowering of our True Self appears.

Beginning in the dark womb,
with patience and loving care,
we prepare for the Spring to come.

MAKING SPACE
Madhavi Glick

Here I place You
in this inadequate place:
small and dark
with dust and grime.
With Sri Guru's help
it will be cleansed over time.

Here I ask You:
please come and rest
I will diligently clean,
removing all other creepers
and overgrown brush.

Here I wait,
night after night,
day after day
for Your sweet arrival
to this awful place.

Here I stay,
here I remain
cleaning and praying
alone in this place,
again and again.

Here I realize
that I continue to hope
that mercy exists;
that I could be a recipient.

In this place
deep within my heart
a tiny seed grows
waiting for the light
of Your Love.

Planting Seeds
Radha Cornia

Planting seeds
Because he said, In India even a poor man has land.
Grow flowers.
And I thought,
I can plant these seeds, these flowers
Beside my door.

So I press the tiny seeds deep into the soil
Doubting in my heart
That anything so small,
Lifeless,
Can be worth watering.

So you might feel
When you speak to me,
Nurturing that tiny seed—
My faith.
How can any anything so small and lifeless
Be worth watering?

Planting seeds
Sometimes I feel the sun
Across my shoulders
Warm, as the seeds must feel
Deep inside the earth.

And something stirs within.

Universal Form

Sudevi Geary

We rise ground up   hands upon the earth we fell on
this world of names calling the seasons to the living.

Draw water from the melt and see
undress your winter skin   grown thick in the darkness
and if the animal of your body wakes in Spring
with a muscle to run and a tongue for your own blood
run to Him   run to the taste of His sounds, ether-born
through blooming mountain bones
where the burnt oaks of wretched hearts lie broken—
ashes for the seeds of love.

If Summer summons storms into your gut
will your chest open to the skies and pray
for rain   offering the fever of your limbs
for His work, a plough
upon the terrain of your being.
Should the heat of the earth rise through your veins
lay rivers of molten speech upon His altar
all sonnets of longing for drawn for Him
and on long bright nights, hold Him
in the horizon of your sight, live
sleepless for Him.

If Autumn breathes roots
to steady your tumbling skies, bind
the tendrils of your mind to His feet
in quakes of humble loss, crawl from the skin
of what's not known to be in Him and rest
falling hands upon the warm mud of the unknown, caressed

with winds that sing *Nama,*
not mine, not mine.

And when Winter pulls quilts of silence across your throat
when your pulse paints thin lines   between slumber and death
bury inwards, beneath the flesh
to build a fire at your bedrock   cook yourself
an underground ripening of the slow moving soul.
When the dark, cold moon demands:
dream! Dream of Him
walk through frozen forests, blind
and hope to be seen by Him.
When your fingers numb, when you rise and fall
a dancing puppet for the heavens   your body aching
under the weight of your seasons
offer Him your day and your night
empty your lungs in His name
feed Him your hunger.

And if you ever long to see His smiling face
sing to Her,
and She will send Spring.

Spring

Gauri Gopika Devi Dasi

On the edge of flight

Waiting for You,
The ocean within

With the trees
I move
Through every season

Ancient pillars of patience:
Witnesses of Your every wish

Rooted in Your energies,
I gain the skies, at last
Free
I fly to what is me

In the fresh spring breeze,
Awake to the calling within
Your seeds of
Love
Gently sprouting in all that be.

LETTING GO
Jhilmil Breckenridge

when you can tune in
to the present

to the softness of the
persian carpet
under your bare
feet

and the coolness
of the hard
granite floor

when you can observe
yourself as a witness
and just watch
the journey

when you can hear
stories
in silence

when your breath
tells you
all you need
to know

when tiny
drops of water
falling off a leaf
are music

when birdsong
fills you with joy
and lightness

and you can smell
freshly mown grass
as you cross the road

when all that matters
is the now

you will realize
all the pleasures
of the world
are in the grasp
of your hand

and you will
simply

let go

Krishna's Abundant Gifts
Dhama-rupini Devi Dasi

Bright, cheery skies heralds spring:
Caw! Caw! Caw! fills the air as choirs of joyful birds sing.

Cherry blossoms permeate the tranquil atmosphere, gently
    showering the soft earth,
Whilst the ants and busy bugs enjoy traversing the dirt.

The earthy scent fills my being,
In a mood of surrender, I am in bliss by the delights that
    I am seeing.

Dear Krishna, I see you everywhere!
My heart is filled with gratitude and I'm deeply touched by
    your care.

You are so magnanimous you've given many beautiful
    treasures!
In return, I pray as your servant, I can give you immense
    pleasure.

Flower Whispers
Bhakti Lata Dasi

slender and graceful with flared petals, like a lady going to a ball
fireworks of color
considered weeds but look like queens
bold artists who paint petals in broad strokes
tiny painters with tiny portraits
grow out of the filth but are never touched by it
grow in tame rows in gardens and fields
grow out of cracks in cement
and in the windowsills of high-rises
perched in millions of glass vases
or up high in trees
surrounded by guardians of thorns
or moats of lakes
or fierce scents
each and every one who ever lived
opens her mouth
and whispers silent words,
"glorious and beautiful I am
for hours and days,
but offer me to God
and I will live forever."

To Be a Flower for Krishna

Narayani Devi Dasi

In the garden of my heart
I pick round *mogra* flowers
one by one,
putting them in my basket,
giving them to Radha
to make Krishna's garland.

Each flower is one bead
of Hare Krishna's mantra.

When the garland is finished
I will see Krishna and
be with Him.

One by one,
patiently picking—
be satisfied with this service
for Radha.

Each bead
becomes a pearl-like stone
that I throw
in front of me
making a bridge
like Hanuman did,
but my bridge
is taking me home
to Krishna.

Now so many beads, flowers
are showering down on me.
My basket is too small.

I make myself into a basket
to catch all the mercy
falling from above.

I'm still picking the flowers
but they've changed into
Your aspiring servants.
I pick them and
give them to Radha
who makes a garland
for You.

Prayers from a Rose
Tulasi D. Estrella

I used to be the flower
singing by your flute,
I'd open in the moonlight
blooming only for you.
My scent was spread all over
the forest of Vrindavan.
"My beautiful Govinda
Don't let me fall in Maya."

Then one day I forgot
the way your eyes could smile,
and fell onto this world
where nothing could be mine.
I am completely lonely;
my petals almost dry.
Because my heart is torn
I want to see your light.

How many days
will I have to spend
hearing of your glories
while you're so far away?
My eyes can't see you
even if you are here,
I'm feeling separation,
my wilting time is near.

Please stop my suffering,
please cure my fears,

I'm ready to surrender.
I know that you can hear
the prayers from a rose
who forgot you were near.
Forgive me for forgetting
but I love you, my dear.

Lessons from the Gentle Flower

Jai Gaurangi Devi Dasi

Oh, how she blooms!
When the dirt around her told her she was but a seed
Destined to remain in darkness,
She battled the seasons until she felt the warmth
Of the encouraging sun upon her back, coaxing her to grow
And so she persevered through the growing pains:
The rainfalls of tears, the scorching trials and tribulations.
She kept faith in those reassuring rays beaming down from above,
Saturating and nourishing her core.
Then one day, she burst through her shell,
And as her petals unfurled,
Revealing her true self to the world,
She found her identity:
She felt free.

Mandarin Infused

Kitzia Kokopelmana

Beloved…
Your Cosmic presence embraces my soul
The Creation of your unfolding brings me joy
and I don't cease to amuse my senses with your magnificence…
Your mandarin kisses
spiraling in the fragrance of million flowers
make my body dance
in the warm grass
while dragonflies join the fun
buzzing the song of the sunset.
Communing with your love
I welcome the juiciness of your fruits
to make my cells with your beauty.
When your Spirit takes form
on Earth
she blossoms
joy
in the name of nature
and I become the child
and the fairy
that embodies all that you are
as I pray a prayer of a life
well lived.

Recipients

Laura Smith

Oh Light, trickle down

onto the shadowy forest
nooks of our eyelids so
we may see fire dancing
in circles through the trees
even in darkness.

Let Your flames drip heavily

onto our rose garden cheeks so
they may seep into the crevasses
of our petals and nudge them
open to embrace the reflection
of Your palm outstretched, inviting.

Monsoon Rains

Anjali Sharma

Sipping ginger tea
looking outside the window
wondering how time flies past
so quickly, like in dreams.
How many seasons?
How many years have gone by?

Let this flow wherever life takes it!
These pearls of raindrops
falling on my heart;
they pull a string,
a chord inside of me.
God only knows where it goes!

It must be a secret place:
a mystical land, a pretty garden
where one day
I'll watch it rain forever.

Mayapur Storms

Narayani Devi Dasi

Chased home early
From the Ganga
As a storm blows in
From the west.

Gusts of dust
Transform into
Raindrops blowing
Horizontally
As lightning and thunder
Turn a hot sultry sunny day
Into a festival of wind,
Rain, sound and light.

The wind blows strong,
As windows break, doors slam,
And I ask myself,
Why did they make the
Kitchen doors out of glass?

The rain lightens,
Thunder grows distant
The sky brightens,
Yet the wind continues
Only to bring the storm back
From the opposite direction.

And we remember how once
Srila Prabhupada enjoyed
The wind blowing through his room,
And he said,
There's no place like Mayapur!

Monsoon Krishna

Ananda Vrindavan Devi

It is written that the
color of Krishna
is like a monsoon cloud
dark bluish grey
like the heavy rains
gathering at the edge
of an unbearably hot day
or at the edge of an
unbearable time of our life
a low rumbling of cool relief
that we know is going to
change things
change us.
Monsoon Krishna
is known as Syamasundar
the beautiful Syama
the color of love, joy, hope
the color of mystery, movement, and depth
the color of life—rich, full, and ready to overflow
when the cloud bursts
upon us all.

Can we receive?
Can we hold?
Can we stand outside
our protective layers
trusting the goodness
of that dark cloud?
We need to let that happen.
We need to dance and sing

and be swept away in the
monsoon rains of Krishna's love
with joyful abandon.

We need this weather, this rain. We need this love.

Monsoon Man

Krsnaa Mary Devi Dasi Fitch

When it's cloudy
I think of You
The darkness
Becomes sweet
My heart aches
From stinging pain
I gasp for breath
Feeling the long needle of attachment
Being pulled from my heart
Your Love
Is evident
In my life
Every time
You take things away from me
I know that You love me
That You will not be satisfied
With only part of myself
That You want me Entirely
You are a greedy lover
And I am humbled
What painful joy
I feel
Surrendering
And feeling Loved
Yes, you can have me
Wholly
That is what I had asked for before
For You to take me as Your own
With tears in my eyes
I had pleaded
It seems You heard me
And conceded

Yamuna

Krishna Rose

Yamuna-Devi
Won't You sprinkle delight for mine eyes
For I have longed for so long
For your shores…

Paramour of the Lady of my heart
You have lent me a vision of Your pure devotee's eyes
Which despise to glance upon anything impure
So dazed I sit
Dreaming of Your world
The Lotus Whirl
So near
So far
You are
Enthroned in this heart made of stone
Not bone
For bone is too easily broke…

Only Thee

Ananda Shakti

My heart is like a river
Its currents being drawn to Your deep waters
This river longs to be merged with Your ocean of madhu
Where there is only thee my Lord
and no longer me

Sister of Yamaraja

Daya Dhara Devi Dasi

Your divine current flows all around.
Your waters so profound!

The Lotus feet of *All That Is* have been placed on you.
How you shiver when this occurs!

Your waves get bigger as He plays with Radha and Her friends.
But when they are apart, you weep.

Oh! Your tears fill the world with streams of beauty!
By entering your streams, *Love of God* enters the heart.

The great dance on the serpent Kaliya's head
was performed with you as the stage!

The Gopi's dresses were stolen on your banks
where secret pastimes were also enacted.

Oh, Yamuna Devi!
When, oh when, will you be so merciful to this fallen servant?
That I may behold all these things with spiritual vision!

In the Forest of Vrinda

Niscala Dasi

Oh heart! Learn to long for...
Oh mind! Think of...
Their sweet Bhauma lila
And nectar, drink of!

Oh eyes! Yearn to see...
Without foolish blinking!
Their sweet Bhauma lila
It's sweet nectar drinking!

Oh fool! Oh fool!
Why do you forget?
With your foolish desires
You fuss and you fret!

Thousands of boons
Are of no use to me!
May they all go away
And instead may I see...

Enthralled in their lila
Sweet Radha Govinda!
In the moonlit groves
In the forest of Vrinda!

CHAPTER NINE

THE HOLY NAMES

*I look into my heart
and listen to its beating,
saying Your Name,
trying to find my way back;
back to where I belong: with You.*

Jasmine Kang

My Relationship with The Holy Name

Arcana siddhi Devi

Many are the ways that we connect to our world and form relationships: My neighbor's friendly pit bull greets me with her enthusiastic body gyrations as we walk together to the mailbox. A chigger bites my ankle. The honey suckle sweet aroma enters my nostrils. Raindrops from a lonely cloud wet my lips.

Some relationships last only a brief moment while others endure throughout our lifetime. I hold my grandfather's 94 year-old hand—wrinkled, soft skin with protruding veins. He doesn't recognize me anymore—once his favorite little girl in the world. My tears moisten our interlocked fingers. I know it is time to let go. Attachment to things that don't endure is the womb from which suffering is born. I gently slide my hand away from his now sleeping body.

Then there are those relationships, which last as long as we do. In our Bhakti tradition, the connections we form with Sanskrit names of the Divine form one such essential relationship in our lives.

I softly chant names of God that are dear to me: *Hare*, *Krishna* and *Rama*. For four decades I have been developing a relationship with God by chanting these names, sometimes softly to myself and sometimes singing them loudly with others. Whenever I do I feel the Lord's presence in the room—my dearest friend, my ever well wisher. The holy quality of these ancient names becomes sweetly tangible.

Like a street sweeper, the holy names cleanse my heart of lifetimes of material impressions and desires. Depression, anxiety, and bulimia: my mental struggles from the past now seem like distant dreams to me. The holy name leads me by my hand to my real prospect, beyond the banal, the temporary sounds and sights of this world. In that eternal realm every molecule is made of pure loving energy! The lord descends from that place in the form of his name and enters the courtyard of my heart.

Over the years my faith and attraction have increased for chanting these names. Just as when one suffers from jaundice, sugar candy tastes bitter to them, and as our diseased condition improves, sugar tastes sweet again—so the names become sweeter as I regain my spiritual health.

In the following poems, we hear my Bhakti sisters also encounter the sweetness of the holy names, as we are offered glimpses into their own intimate relationships with the mantra at the heart of our Bhakti tradition: *Hare Krishna Hare Krishna Krishna Krishna Hare Hare, Hare Rama Hare rama Rama Rama Hare Hare.*

Contained within the mantra, like a tree inside of a seed, is God's, or Krishna's exquisitely beautiful form, his unlimited qualities and his pastimes. In time, these intimate aspects become revealed to the practitioner who also makes these names dear. For now I feel the presence of God's divine beloved, Radha (*Hare*), and God himself, Krishna, like the warm sun rising on a chilly autumn morning.

The life giving names walk with me, sit with me, sleep with me. Even as my body perishes in the near future, the names will guide me to my next destination. The names will continue to soften my stone like heart until it melts into loving ecstasy for the personalities who own the names that I chant.

Spark

Dhanya Rico

I am lost
In a dense wood
Of my mind's planting.
The leaves have fallen,
What once offered shelter
Now only blocks the light.

A fire must burn.
A natural cleanse
Keeps the forest alive.
A self-imposed
Extinction
Of all that is ready to go.
Lifetimes of habit
Sinking roots deep in the mud
Too strong to pull,
The fire must come.
I close my eyes
Let the flame be lit
My tongue and the Name
Are the flint and the steel
I try
I try
I try… a spark.
A prayer, a light, a warmth.
I fan the spark
And it begins to catch.

Mantra Lullaby
Kadamba Mala Devi Dasi

sometimes I wonder
if you remember
when you were
little
and just learning to sleep
alone in your own bed,
how I would sing
hare krishna
to you
in a certain tune—
one that I cannot describe
without singing,
but that if I close my eyes
I can hear in his
voice
as he sang it
on the pilgrimage path
in the holy place
with his arms raised up
hands to the sky
swaying back and forth
as we walked,
bare feet,
praying
praying
being careful
what we asked for,
singing in response
in this tune
that felt like the warmest embrace.

and so I sang it to you,
years later,
trying to give you the same
solace,
like in *The Giver*
when Jonas soothed
baby Gabe
with memories
of the waves lapping,
I was there
rubbing your back
softly
singing
that mantra lullaby
comforting
us both.

Ode to the Holy Name

Jahnavi Harrison

Whisper it beneath the summer oaks
while swallows dive above
Shout it in your morning shower,
share it with the ones you love.
Sing it loud, groups of ten,
three or seventy-five,
brand it on your beating chest and
keep your heart alive.
In the garden, on the bus,
before exams and interviews,
at joyous birth and bitter death,
sing this name, loud and true.
Call it when your days are long,
breathe it in and out with heavy head,
cry it over your morning tea,
and into your pillow before bed.
Wash this name through every fibre,
rinse and repeat, rinse and repeat
sing with everything you have,
soft, sweet, subtle, deep.

On the Beads of Love, I Chant Your Name

Promila Chitkara

Some beats of my heart sing your name
Some wander away to the world of trivial matters
All beats but belong to you
Through me you orchestrate
Some times they rebel, some times they obey

Mantra's Embrace

Krishna Kanta Dasi

On full moon nights,
  when my heart is a glutton for aching,
    and obscurity devours my mind,
      and my brokenness reaches
        for the chocolate truffles,
          I hear it beckoning…
        louder than laundry and dirty dishes,
      or even the threats of imported fears
    tucked between yawning wounds
  and a famished spirit,
and that stubborn feeling that I don't belong:
this mantra-meditation calls me.
Decorated with sonic diamonds
  straight from the treasure chest of antiquity
    trickling down through the ages
      like honey dripping from hives in the summer
      a thousand sparkling jewels for my soul
        swirling, deliciously, with primordial rhythms:
      which soothe and comfort,
    and rock me in their arms like a mother
    forgetting trauma that nestles in the physical
  I chant upon a bridge to the spiritual
as this mantra likes to dance on my tongue.
Mending consciousness with stitches of sound,
  gently quilting serenity into my cells,
    like fine embroidery of endorphin threads
      onto a pillow of consciousness
        a festival of color brighter than spring blossoms.
         For, my soul picnics
    in these flowering fields

   found at the edges of eternity,
    where I construct coffins for my anxieties,
  every time I take to chanting.
Forget the movies and chocolates!
That hollow glitter that taunts my heart
  when loneliness whines.
    Instead, I am captured by medicinal melodies:
   suns that rise in the dark,
    so my reflection is clear,
     so I see myself again
    in the dew drops of my morning meditation
   in the mirrors of this mantra,
  that holds me more completely
than anything else ever will, or could.
For this sound is made of pure love!
One in substance with my own being
and way sweeter than any truffle.

Mending My Heart
Ananta Devi Dasi

Endless Tragedies, heartbreaks
You are there
Picking up the fragments
Sewing and mending me
With your Mercy threads
Quilting the path
Gently leading me
Right to You
To Lord Chaitanya
To Radha-Krishna
Glimpses of the Divine
Cleansing the debris
Clearing teary eyes
Shining into the light of my heart
Your smile
Eternally blissful
Courageously armed
Uplifting the Torchlight of Knowledge
Truth Flowing
Igniting Peace
Holy Name
Joy Dance
Unlimitedly embracing
Arms open high
Motivating mission strength
Receiving signals
I follow forward
One step
Then the other
By your mercy...

Seduce this Soul

Radha Cornia

Seduce this soul
My black-eyed Lord
Woo me from the wayward path of sin
Let my heart fall victim to
The curling locks of silk soft hair
That brush against Your chin

Seduce this soul
Shyamasundara
Drowning in an ocean of the dead
Let my eyes be conquered by
The gently waiving peacock plume
You wear upon Your head.

Seduce this soul
Eternal Youth
Win me from material domain
My ears forever ravished by
A subtle, mystic melody
The chanting of Your name.

Holy Name
Braja Sorensen

your love dances in my heart
swings in rapturous twirls
its form of silent grace
frolics where no one sees…

but I do

its gossamer skirts
lift and swirl as we spin
whirling in rhythm
and then it becomes

my breath

When I Just Sit and Chant
Mohini Madhavi Devi Dasi

When I just sit and chant my mind seems to declare:
"Yes, I am in my home! I'm secure, my soul is now bare!"
The material world temporarily disappears,
As do my problems, my pains and my fears.

When I just sit and chant, worthy rivers of tears flow
When I just sit and chant, I feel the love you bestow!
A smile appears on my face, for this heart beats with joy
Oh, no words can explain, that feeling I feel
That Krishna's Name is real!
when I just sit and chant.

When I just sit and chant, I try to focus my all
on hearing each name, inside my heart's call
Sounds that send all other thoughts away!
First Hare, then Krishna…nothing else can stay.
When I just sit and chant the Holy Name is at play.

When I just sit and chant, I try to cry from within
as Krishna's mercy upon little me makes my tiny soul spin
"Oh dear One, please hear me! Awaken my love!"
When I just sit and chant I wear my prayers like a glove.

When I just sit and chant, my tongue dances for His pleasure
I feel myself expressing: "You are my treasure!"
"Oh Gopinath! Your little servant is here calling out!"
When I just sit and chant rain quenches my heart's drought.

A Prayer
Vrindvani Dasi

I
wish to be
abandoned.
Remove the mask, stop the show
Listen:

my soul sobs
Your names.

Bail

Alexandra Moga

like a fortune trapped beneath
the letters of the law
a truth yearns to make it out of this
prison-house of thought
my lips,
dutiful civil servants
they call on the whispers of the heart
and giving voice to mercy,
and lending inspiration to reason
post bail posthaste
just by speaking of You

Your Name

Jasmine Kang

Sweet is Your Name bliss
and the smile on Your face
with eyes that shine brightly
Oh, how they shine
and take me away!
It all makes me smile
to say Your Name.

Like a rose drenched in honey
my heart is drenched in this Love;
Such sweetness never fades,
it is the nectar I kiss
as I find bliss in Your Name:
Your Name bliss.

They say the journey is long,
but you can find the way.
Sometimes you feel lost
and don't know what to do,
but there is a way
oh, there is a way:
Your Name is the way…
The only way.

In the light of Your eyes
I see shining
and find there is truth, love and beauty
hidden away deep within
in the heart of all being.

Your eyes shine true
and Your flute sings sweetly
like the fragrance of a flower
calling me to it.
Just say the Name!
Oh, say the Name!

I look into my heart
and listen to its beating
saying Your Name,
trying to find my way back;
back to where I belong: with You.

Oh, just show me the way!
Fill me with the Love of You!
Shower me with it
and take me back to You:
Where my heart is: with You.

THERE

Kathamrita Devi Dasi

Here You are
You are here with me
and everywhere has become You
You are everything!
And besides this, there is nothing
but more You.
And loneliness is myself feeling separate from You
although I am but a tiny part of you
apart from you I cannot be.
In the distance within my heart
there is only enough space
for Your hands to extend
into nowhere You cannot reach.
You are everywhere, but within my mind…
Still, that is You pretending to hide
in the place I hide myself.
Still, You are there in all that stuff:
making up the particles of every speck of dust
and the time it will take for all my dreams to rust.
To fill my mind with You
would make every moment full
for You are every moment eternally…still.
In that stillness, I feel You moving
I wish to come along
I'll sing to You a sacred tune
Your name in every song.
And for everyone You are,
and in every heart You keep a secret
safe—although forgotten
of a Lover ever-sweet.

To sing Your name: intoxicatingly pure
is to hear Your heart within my heart.
There You are
and here You are too
Oh Krishna You are present!
And in Your name I hear You.

Kirtan Forever!

Mohini Madhavi Devi Dasi

This *kirtan* makes me spin in a circle,
feel like flying to the sky and smile for its entire duration!
This *kirtan* makes me feel light and makes me jump,
It makes me happy so that I sing loudly, again and again!

The sound of *mridanga* drum enters both of my ears
And *karatals* intensify the singing of the Holy Names
through *mangala arati, tulasi puja,* and then 8 verses
Oh these mornings, these *kirtans*! Let them last forever!

Later, three o'clock arrives and tempts me to sleep
but instead I bathe, put *tilak* on, wrap myself in a sari
and run to the temple to be seen by Gopinath!
For I want His pleasure to escalate higher than before
when He hears my prayers, and watches me dance in *kirtan*.

I dance and spin in a circle of gratitude to Srila Prabhupada
and to all of my other Gurus!
Thanking them and Gopinath for giving me life!
For giving me chance to live forever!
I can't repay them. I do not have enough treasure!
But at least beg I can beg:
That they help me make my whole life
a source of Their pleasure:
Kirtan Forever!

A Ratha Yatra Meditation

Yasomati Devi Dasi

What can I do when my heart is breaking?
When each cell is calling Your name?
All people around are singing,
I am putting my head down in shame.
Hiding my tears. Don't let them see,
that I cannot find another way to be
than at your feet, getting lost in Your eyes,
Guarding your door…when the whole universe cries
I cry with it, waiting for YOU.

Captured

Seva-mayi Dasi

Like a net that is cast into a furious sea
Your love captures my drowning devotion
And guides it to rise above the swelling tide.
Upon the rays of the ascending sun my soul's
song cries out to You. It is one of simple surrender.
Oh Radha, let us dance in the shimmer of dewdrops
that adorn the grass below His lotus feet.
May our hearts be encircled by the melodies of His
flute's enchanting song,
drawing us ever deeper into His embrace.
Sister, guide me home to His love as I sing Your name
and His, to the Cosmos bending low in recognition
of His glorious transcendence. Krishna is everywhere.
Between every atom the truth of His being emanates;
inviting all souls to dance in the rasa of His Divine love.
Ushering all souls in to surrender and return back home
to the shores of eternal devotion.
Oh, son of Yashoda and Nandana, divine lover of the Gopis,
You have ensnared my heart playfully.
Letting it go at times, oh merciful Govinda,
you allow it to wander and then once again draw
back your bow string and let lose the arrows of Your love
to pierce my soul deep, wounding it in Your mercy
with the unbearable pangs of separation.
My heart flees from the material and to its only true remedy,
Until all that seems to exist is the transcendental tonic of
Your Holy names:
Hare Krishna, Hare Krishna Krishna Krishna Hare Hare
Hare Rama, Hare Rama Rama Rama Hare Hare

Lord Krishna's Glorious Holy Name

Krishna Priya Dasi

Chant the holy name when sad and gloomy:
It will dry up all your tears.
If you're alone and scared
it will take away all your fears.

Chant when tense and worried,
for the holy name helps you to cope.
If life seems void and dry,
The Name showers the rain of hope.

When strangled by the weeds of material life,
The Holy Name will uproot them automatically!
If you chant when pained by lonely silence,
the Name will resound ecstatically.

If disturbed about the things you do
and about those with whom you associate,
you may feel desolate and alone,
but the Supreme is with Whom you can communicate:

Hare Krishna, Hare Krishna
Krishna Krishna Hare Hare
Hare Rama, Hare Rama
Rama Rama Hare Hare

The *maha mantra* is empowered
to end all life's confusions.
Even chanted just one time,
it destroys all of your delusions.

Seeds of Liberation

Meenakshi

Open the door tonight to spaciousness:
vast, free and with painted crimson beauty.

This space inside… this energy…
is meant to be awakened
and express its song
with every gust of wind of the soul.

Let it blow
through every inhale, every exhale,
and all the places in between.

There are myriad different ways to kiss the ground.
And a million different ways to embrace the sky.

If we turn our head down to our dancing feet
and lift our gaze high to our angels above
we can know the secrets the ancient ones knew,
and live by them.

Let's turn our collective nightlights ON
and see through the darkness,
and watch the shifting tides of all of life's stories,
as we sit inside the fortress of freedom.

Here we plant the seeds of liberation with each "Hari bol!"

Dancing God

Paraschiva Florescu

His name comes out in a cry:
Krishna
Krishna
Krishna
My mouth rolls with anticipation.

Look how He dances on my tongue;
how with each step He presses His soft sole
into my skin; rising in ecstasy,

and He rolls on the edge of my heart:
from His hands mercy flowing like rivers.

I yearn for Him to find me,
pull me up from the back of my neck
place me on His chest,
father-like, with warmth.

This time I will not leave,
for I have known darkness and strangers.
Enough, enough!

Now He comes home:
a golden pulse of life, unmovable light
He watches

and I catch His tears and make them my own
as He becomes the space of silence,
the unspoken words and happenings of my life.
As He becomes sweet taste on my lips
the soft turning of time.

On my tongue
He dances, dances, dances
and never stops.

Nothing More to Say

Krsnaa Mary Devi Dasi Fitch

Hare Krishna
My mother sang to me
As I listened in the womb
Hare Krishna
People said
When they heard this baby croon
Hare Krishna
I sang
In my tiny child voice
Hare Krishna
I was told
Is the best and only choice
Hare Krishna
I heard
But decided to ignore
Hare Krishna
Sometimes I saw it as a bore
Hare Krishna
It's hard to forget You and enjoy
Hare Krishna
I love to get & give affection to this boy
Hare Krishna
Reminded me of my innocent past
Hare Krishna
My life, seemed was going by so fast
Hare Krishna
Is what I said, when my stomach turned to knots
Hare Krishna
Is what I screamed when I felt that I was lost
Hare Krishna

Is what I chanted when the pain wouldn't go away
Hare Krishna
Though I'm fallen, You uplifted me anyway
Hare Krishna
Seems my only real companion in this life
Hare Krishna
Even if I never again become a wife
Hare Krishna
Shines in front of my eyes full of tears
Hare Krishna
You begin to wash away all my fears
Hare Krishna
I pray, to hear You every day
Hare Krishna
From my heart, I chant
because there's nothing more to say
But…
Hare Krishna Hare Krishna Krishna Krishna Hare Hare
Hare Rama Hare Rama Rama Rama Hare Hare

NOTE ON STYLE AND SPELLING OF NAMES

The Vaishnava traditions revolve around sacred sounds and their power to illuminate consciousness and awaken love for the Supreme Divine. As such, those who join the tradition—or are born into it—are given ancient Sanskrit names with the potential to do so. We have chosen not to engage the transliteration system of presenting Sanskrit names and words in English. Rather, we have adopted the phonetic spellings of Sanskrit words for easy reading. However, some authors have chosen to use the unusual transliteration spellings of their Sanskrit names with the diacritic marks omitted. For example, this phonetic spelling of "Krishna", would appear as "Krsna" as a transliteration spelling without the diacritic marks (excluding the diacritic under-dots for the *r*, the *s*, and the *n*). Thus the spelling/representation of the author's names is presented here with these inconsistencies.

The only exception is that that all the instances of "Devi" and "Dasi" have been capitalized, as they are part of the author's names. In the Chaitanya Vaishnava lineage the name given by one's guru always ends in "Das" (for men) and "Dasi" (for women) meaning loving servant. When the disciple is female, "Dasi" is often preceded by "Devi", meaning Goddess or goddess-like. For this reason, the names in the "About the Authors" which follows appear in alphabetical order according to *first names*. Additionally, when a name is followed by (ACBSP) it means that that person has received *brahmin* initiation from Abhay Charan Bhaktivedanta Swami Prabhupada, the founder of the Hare Krishna Movement and has requested that they be identified as such.

Many of the participants in this anthology have two names: a legal name and a Sanskrit name given to them by their spiritual teacher, or guru. The attempt has been made by the editors to have all authors' names appear in the book exactly as per each of the individual author's requests. Some use their legal name, others the name their guru gave them, while others have requested that we present both their legal, and guru-given names, or a combination of the two.

ABOUT THE AUTHORS

Akarsini Radhika Devi Dasi: I started practicing Krishna Consciousness in Southern Italy when I was 19. I spent most of my life serving and residing in ISKCON temple communities. I never attempted writing poetry until I was inspired to give a special offering for my guru's birthday and poetry just came to my mind.

Alexandra Moga uses poetry and yoga to express and connect with the spiritual spark. Introduced to yoga at a young age, she has been practicing for over 15 years and rhyming lines for most of her conscious life. After 4 years at a culinary arts academy and 5 years of life and art studies in Paris, she sought to deepen her knowledge of yoga. Having completed trainings in Ashtanga, children's, Bhakti and Kundalini Yoga, she now lives in New York where she teaches yoga, writes, and serves on the board of the Foundation for Inspired Living and Supersoul Farm. She is grateful for the teachers and students who enable her to learn and serve on this path.

AnandaRupa Devi Dasi is a Bhakti yoga practitioner, writer, and lover of poetry and short stories. She is interested in Bhakti books, spirituality, and nature. She and her husband are both professional trainers and coaches. Anjujai@gmail.com

Ananda Shakti: Though I was born in Toronto, these days India in my second home. I teach yoga and train yoga teachers at Sananda Yoga and offer Core Pattern Life readings, as well as lead a devotional music group Love Power. When encountering the teachings of yoga I delighted in hearing stories of love overcoming all difficulties were told, and I felt like I had discovered the highest truth possible. When service and love were put before any other wisdom, I cried and melted into a pool of love. I had little interest in the intellectual conversations that were a popular way of understanding the teachings, my answer to difficulties would always be to remember Love, read a poem, or sing. Then I discovered the stories of Krishna and knew I was home.

Ananda Vrindavan Devi is the President of the ISKCON Krishna Temple in Washington DC. She is an educator by profession, and a writer and speaker by interest and inspiration. Her leadership direction is nourished by the 6 Gita Values, the practice of Bhakti, and the writings of the great poets and thinkers through the ages.

Ananta Devi Dasi (Angela Roix) has been writing poetry since she was a young girl. Fascinated with spirituality and nature, poetry has always been a creative outlet for her. She loves writing poetry for her Guru Maharaj, HH Prahladananda Swami. She currently lives in Orlando, Florida with her three sons. She is a Community Business Development Manager for Barnes & Noble, Social Media Coordinator for Ayurbeauty Wellness Center, Sunday School Assistant Teacher, and an aspiring servant of the Lord and His devotees.

Anjali Sharma lives in Mumbai and works in finances there. She has been practicing Reiki for ten years and it was her Reiki teacher and guru who introduced her to Bhakti yoga. Anjali is married to a disciple of Radhanatha Swami, and holds a deep appreciation within her heart for the Holy Land of Vrindavan. She wishes to serve the Lord with love, and extend that love to others in a healing capacity. Anjali believes that chanting is the best medicine and that whatever we are looking for is already inside of us. Bhakti, according to Anjali, is seeing God in every person and being a good human being through whichever practice one follows.

Anuradha Keshavi Devi Dasi has grown up in Dubai, United Arab Emirates. She completed her Bachelors in Engineering from Georgia Tech University in Atlanta, USA. She started her Bhakti journey in 2003 and has been steadily encouraged by her spiritual teachers namely H.H Jayapataka Swami and H.H Radhanath Swami. She currently resides in Dubai, UAE with her family participating in the vibrant community of kirtans and Bhakti practitioners. You may connect with Anuradha Keshavi via her blog: walksatdawn.blogspot.com

Anuradha Sakhi Devi Dasi grew up in the shelter of temples and the philosophy of the Bhakti tradition. Loving guidance from her parents, friends, mentors, and gurus has empowered and inspired her to write about her experiences. She works as a family doctor and is a mother to three children.

Aradhana Devi Dasi (Ainsley Bresnahan) began practicing Bhakti yoga at 15 and later took shelter of her Guru Maharaja, Swami BV Tripurari, at 16. She is currently studying Psychology in hopes of eventually counseling devotees. In addition to her schooling, she writes articles for *The Harmonist* and is an active participant in her Guru's project, *Saragrahi*, a devotee community located near Asheville, North Carolina.

Arcana siddhi Devi has been a Bhakti practitioner since 1976. She is a psychotherapist with her master's degree in social work. In her private practice, she combines tools from psychotherapy and her spiritual practice to address the needs of the whole person-body, mind, and spirit. She and her husband currently live in a rural community in North Carolina. They are both authors, counselors, and teachers.

Atmesvari Dasi was born in Spain. She grew up in the Vaishnava tradition and studied in Gurukulas, spiritual schools in different countries. She is the happy mother of her six-year-old boy son and spends her days raising him. As a creative personality, Atmesvari dedicates as much time as she can to the arts, photography, her love of nature and acquiring knowledge of the self.

Bhakti Lata Dasi fell in love with the written word as a child and has kept a journal, written stories, studied English, and shared blog posts throughout her life. Born and raised in the Bhakti tradition, her writing expresses her longings for meaning and love.

Braja Sorensen is an author, poet, photographer, *bhakti-yogini*, cook, and cow lover, hailing from the beaches of Australia but living on the banks of the sacred Ganges River in Mayapur, West Bengal, since the turn of the century. *Lost & Found in India* (Hay House International, 2013) was her first mainstream book, and she has other published works in the Vaishnava genre: *18 Days: Sri Panca-tattva's Mayapur-lila* (2004), *India & Beyond: Plane Reading for Part-time Babajis* (2012), plus a book of collected writings, *Mad & Divine* (2015). Braja also worked for some years on *Nava-vraja-mahima* (Lal Publishing, 2013) penned by Sivarama Swami, a nine-volume treatise on the sacred land of India through the Vaishnava perspective of pastime, pilgrimage, and philosophy. Her first poetry book, *Tryst: Ghazals of Love*, is due to be published in 2016, along with her first fiction novel, *Of Noble Blood*. *Yoga in the Gita* is the first collaborative work of many to come with writing partner Catherine Ghosh. Connect with her via Facebook, or her website: brajasorensen.com

Champak Manjari Dasi

Daya Dhara Devi Dasi is a 27-year old aspiring spiritual activist from California who finds simplicity in writing and exploring her creativity. This extends into poetry, music and day-to-day activities. Through her spiritual cultivation of Bhakti yoga, she has found that one of the best ways to commune with the Supreme is to co-create and allow the divine presence to inspire and lead her into deeper depths of discovery.

Debra Sue Lynn is a published author, poet, lecturer, actress, and life-teacher. Originally raised in Judaism, she began a personal practice of Bhakti yoga in 1985. Debra is a Certified EFT Practitioner, Reiki Master, and Ordained Spiritual Minister. She published *Tales from the Heart* a book of short stories, poems of love, fantasy, heartbreak, and Haiku. Debra sponsors and judges a poetry contest yearly through The Indiana State Poetry Federation and leads an 87-member poetry group via AllPoetry.com. Debra resides in Flagler Beach, Florida. Her website is healingatyourfingertips.com

Devasri Radhika Devi Dasi (Devahitu Shaw) is a lawyer, photographer, animal rights activist, Indian classical music student, and writer. The author has grown up in India exploring different religious and spiritual movements. As a lawyer, communication is her skill. She believes poetry and women have an ancient and deep relationship; hence poetry is the expression of the heart.

Devesani Radhika Dasi: I am a disciple of His Holiness Jayapataka Swami. I grew up in the New Talavana Farm Community in Carriere, Mississippi, USA. When I was 15, I moved to Sridham Mayapur in order to study in the girls' gurukula. After graduating, I got married and continued to do serve in the gurukula as a teacher and secretary. Now, years later, by Gauranga's mercy, I still live in Mayapur with my husband and daughter, where I have the great fortune of assisting in the annual, year-long preparation of the Chandan Yatra festival for Sri Sri Radha Madhava.

Dhama-rupini Devi Dasi: I am a disciple of His Holiness Guru Prasad Swami. I'm originally from Trinidad and migrated to Vancouver in 2010. I was a former High School Teacher and taught ESL students. I am currently focusing on raising my young children ages 2 and 4. I serve as the principal of ISKCON Vancouver's Sunday school. I have also written three devotional children's books: *Gajendra*, *Hari's Adventure in Port- of- Spain* and *Hanuman*. Join me on my website: www.juliarambharose.com and Facebook page Lotus Creations Publication.

Dhanya Rico was born in Caracas, Venezuela. She was raised in a multicultural household, which encouraged spirituality and creative exploration. After studying the ancient philosophy of the Bhakti tradition in Mayapur, India, she returned with a renewed sense of purpose: uniting her devotional practice with her creative talents as an offering to God. She has traveled the world sharing her music, collaborating with and supporting other artists, and spreading the message of the Bhakti faith. In 2015, she received both Master's and Specialist's degrees in Marriage and Family Therapy. She lives in Alachua, Florida with her husband, Bali Rico.

Gandarvika Devi Dasi (Kelly Fowler) was an exemplary mother, wife, spiritual guide, friend, and devotee of Krishna from San Diego, CA. There, she served in many capacities over the years, including temple president, naturally endearing herself to the community with her happy demeanor. She also served the Dallas and Alachua ISKCON communities. For the last 12 years, she and her husband Mahahari Das started a temple in Buenos Aires, including a thriving restaurant, a well-attended Sunday school and a cooking school. She left her body on May 25th in Buenos Aires, Argentina, listening to Srila Prabhupada chanting while surrounded by friends and family.

Gauri Gopika Devi Dasi has been a practitioner of Bhakti yoga since 2011 and started writing poetry in her teenage years as a mean of expression and a search for purpose in life. It remains an enriching element to her spiritual practice.

Gloriana Amador Aguero: I was born in Costa Rica in 1987. I studied art and visual communication with an emphasis on painting, which led me to managing museum collections and archives of modern and contemporary art. I am also a member of the Board of Directors of the Costa Rican Committee of the International Counsel of Museums. I cultivate Bhakti through the arts, singing, drawing and poetry, and have received much of my inspiration from my stay in Vrindavan, India, where I felt deeply called by Krishna's love. I am doing independent studies at the Bhaktivedanta College Online.

Gopalpreet Taya Malakian is a poet, artist and yogini living in Nevada City, Ca. Her spiritual name, Gopalpreet, means "Beloved of the Divine" which brought tears to her eyes upon receiving, as her life has been lead by a deep devotion for the Sacred. Her poetry, artwork, yoga and meditation offerings can be explored at www.tiffanaya.com

Gopi Gita Schomaker is Mom to her boys, Vraja and Nitai, and wife to steady Rupa. As Vice Principal of TKG Academy, Srila Prabhupada's first school, she dreams of a time where every child can connect the power of words to their heart's Beloved. She regularly escapes to poetry's calling.

Gopika-kanta Dasi is a public school teacher in New Jersey. Her passion for education extends beyond her career. Gopika also directs the Sunday School and facilitates leadership classes for the youth in her local ISKCON community. Writing poetry helps support Gopika in her quest to serve the local community and deepen her spiritual practice.

Gopi Kumari Devi Dasi is a disciple of Radhanatha Swami and currently resides in New York City. She works as a Psychiatric Nurse Practitioner and regularly serves at the Bhakti Center. She was raised in the Catholic tradition and met the devotees in April 2009 while attending college at the University of Maryland. Gopi Kumari shares her work in this book as an offering to her beloved Gurudeva and prays for continuous service to him.

Hladini Shakti Devi Dasi: I have been working with horses in Florida since 2011. In the winter of 2014, a friend suggested that I participate in a Satvatove seminar to improve my horse riding. I entered the seminar room identifying myself as a veterinarian atheist from Czech. After a few days of attending the seminar facilitated by Dhira Govinda and Malini, a desire appeared in my heart to serve God. Although I didn't know what it meant at the time, I left the seminar with Srila Prabhupada's Bhagavad Gita. The rest is history!

Indu Arora is an Ayurveda and Yoga Therapist based out of USA. Her teachings are deeply rooted in her philosophy: 'Nothing has the greatest power to heal, but Self.' She is a celebrated author of "Mudra: The Sacred Secret" and "Yoga—Ancient Heritage, Tomorrow's Vision". When not traveling, she lives in Minneapolis. www.induarora.com

Jagattarini Dasi

Jahnavi Harrison was raised in a family of Bhakti yoga practitioners at Bhaktivedanta Manor in England. She is trained in dance, music, writing and visual arts, and aspires to utilize these abilities to uplift, empower, and inspire others. She writes regularly for print and broadcast media including for BBC Radio 2's 'Pause for Thought', and her blog 'The Little Conch'.

Jahnavi Priya Dasi: I live in Surat, India and am a disciple of Bhakti Charu Swami. I love reading Srimad Bhagavatam, writing and teaching others about Krishna. I am mother to two daughters who I love very much. They are my favorite company!

Jai Gaurangi Devi Dasi: I was born as Jaanki Govindia and raised in the suburbs of London. The seed of devotion was sown in my heart by my dear parents and later nourished by my spiritual master Radhanath Swami. My journey of self-discovery in Bhakti yoga has been greatly influenced by my relationship with poetry and prose. I see writing as an offering of my heart to the world; sharing the expressions of my soul through my pen gives me a deep connection to the hearts of others exploring this journey of life alongside me. In the words of the great Mother Teresa, "I am a little pencil in the hand of a writing God, who is sending a love letter to the world."

Jai Radhika Devi Dasi recently escaped the corporate world to become a serious student of Bhakti. She traveled to India where she met Radhanath Swami and became his disciple. She currently resides at *Bhaktivana*, a small Krishna conscious community, outside of Baldwin, Kansas.

Janavi Held started writing poetry and wandering around with her father's camera as a child. At the age of nineteen, she began practicing Bhakti yoga. She holds a bachelor's degree from Goddard College where she studied poetry, photography and media studies. She is the author of Letters to My Oldest Friend (June, 2017), a book of poetry and photography.

Jasmine Kang is a poet who found herself through Bhakti yoga. She shares her reflections and expressions from the heart through prose and poetry. While her passion lies in art and creative writing, music, and nature inspire her. To read more of Jasmine's poetic work, visit her website Moonshinegarden.com.

Jen Walls is a devoted author/international poet/literary reviewer/critic; bringing joyful heart's radiance; pulsating us deeply within a loving personality of rare positivity. She has authored two poetry collections: *The Tender Petals* (Nov. 2014, Inner Child Press) and *OM Santih Santih Santih—Love and Peace Duet Poetry* (Nov. 2015, The Poetry Society of India), which combined divine nature inspired spiritual duet poems. Jen's peace-filled poetry vibrates alive inside many print and electronic anthologies across the globe, including USA, UK, Africa, and India. Her poetic contributions lovingly promote world peace and global harmony, and have thus earned Jen the 2016 Distinguished Poet Award from Writers International Network (WIN-Canada). She resides in Saint Paul, Minnesota, USA with her loving family.

Jennieke Janaki was born in the Netherlands She traveled the world as a model and found her peace and true Home when taking her first yoga class in 1989. Initiated into the Sivananda Lineage, Janaki founded Sharanam Yoga in 2006, with the mission "Healing through Surrender" where she teaches both adults and children. Janaki is author of a poetry collection "Divine Sweetness: Love Aspirations."

Jhilmil Breckenridge is a poet, writer, and activist. She is passionate about issues of women, disability, and mental health. Jhilmil is currently working on a Ph.D. in Creative Writing from the University of Central Lancashire. She is the Founder of Bhor, a charity in New Delhi, which works in the field of mental health advocacy. Jhilmil is a *yogini* and a *pranic* energy practitioner. Follow her at @jhilmilspirit on Twitter.

Jvalamukhi Devi Dasi (Jvala Kopecka) is a second-generation Hare Krishna devotee, a Gurukuli, now 41 years old. Her mother Mrgaksi wrote the songs many devotees know called the *Little Vaisnava Songs*. She and her three siblings still have the burning passion to express Krishna Consciousness through the arts. Jvala has a beautiful husband of 18 years, three boys, dogs, a garden, and a full time job healing herself and others. Doing cosmic battle inside and out, she spends her days mothering, cleaning, cooking, singing, crying, and begging Lord Krishna for the true Sankirtan movement to emerge from the overtaken organization. Much pain and hope in this regard is expressing in her songs, poetry, writings, and videos. Her deepest desire is for sincere spiritual seekers to have the real treasure that our beloved Srila Prabhupada came to give the world, and to manifest a Vedic Arts school before her kids grow up!

Kadamba Mala Devi Dasi also known as Mala Gutierrez is a wife, mother of two daughters, poet, Bhakti *yogini*, and teacher of high school and college writing and literature. She is the author of a collection of poems titled *"...and other poems."* More information can be found at teaormebooks.com.

Kaivalya Sundari Devi Dasi: A disciple of Jayapataka Swami since 1983, I have been serving New Talavan in Mississippi, U.S.A. I have taught in the New Talavan Gurukula, raised two children—now adults and initiated members of ISKCON—and continue to perform deity dressing and other priestly activities. With the responsibilities of Grihastha life, I find myself drawn towards sharing Krishna Consciousness with others via photography, parenting, and grandmotherhood.

Kathamrita Devi Dasi: My relationship to my poetry is much like the way people speak to a therapist, or a best friend. It's my confidential talks with my own heart, or my hearts revelations reaching realization in my mind or beyond it. It is my ability to extend to others through words, my deepest emotions, needs, or questions. It is my voice to the world, and for all to see. A bare boned, raw and unrefined vision of my own imperfections, dancing towards eternity.

Kelly Noyes was born and raised in Birmingham Michigan, a suburb of Detroit. She studied nursing at the University of Michigan. Over time she found her passion in hospice, a field in which she finds deeply rewarding. She is a loving mother to her daughter. She finds joy in nature, art, music, mantra, yoga, and dance. In her spare time, she enjoys writing, traveling, meditating, and continuing on the journey within and without. She currently resides in Auburn Hills Michigan.

Kitzia Kokopelmana travels between Baja California, Mexico and the Andean Mountains in Ecuador where in her devotion to the Divine she crafts rich botanical garden sites of as much beneficial diversity as she can find. Her first love was literature, which she began to express in her native language of Spanish, publishing her earliest poems in the local newspapers at age 13. With time, her romance with poetry has deepened. As a prolific writer she loves to bring the history of things and the esoteric concepts to life through poetry and storytelling.

Krishna Kanta Dasi (Catherine L. Schweig) has been practicing Bhakti yoga since 1986, and was initiated into the Chaitanya Vaishnava tradition in 1990 by Srila Bhakti Prappan Damodar Goswami in India. Passionate about inspiring women to honor their voices, she founded the "Vaishnavi Voices Poetry Project". In 2012 Krishna Kanta started the "Journey of the Heart: Women's Spiritual Poetry" online community, for which she has edited and published four anthologies of women's writings. She is mother to two grown sons and lives in Virginia with her partner, Garuda, with whom she co-founded "The Secret Yoga Institute". She also loves nature and makes vegan, Waldorf-style dolls. Catherine@secretyoga.com

Krishna Priya Dasi is a disciple of His Holiness Lokanath Swami and was born in Rajasthan, India. She paints traditional Rajasthani art and writes devotional poems and cookbooks. Her painting titled *Rasa-Lila* graces the front cover of *Dance of Divine Love* by Graham M. Schweig and her poetry book, *Lotus Lyrics* was inspired by His Divine Grace A.C. Bhaktivedanta Swami's *Bhagavad-gita As It Is*. Krishna Priya has been cooking for the Deities, Sri Sri Radha Golokananda, at the ISKCON temple in Hillsborough, North Carolina since 1996. Desirous of sharing her personal recipes with others, she compiled *The Art of Indian Sweets* and *Devotional Dishes*. She is presently working on a new series of cookbooks. www.Lotuslyrics.com

Krishna Rose: Born in Hertfordshire, England, Krishna has been deeply moved by classic poetry, art and music. After many years of traveling the world in the music industry working with famous rock artists, she took a life-changing trip to India, where she met her spiritual teacher Srila Bhaktivedanta Narayana Goswami Maharaja, who told her to write and perform English songs in the vein of great poets like Wordsworth, Yeats and Milton. As such she self-produced four albums: *Beneath The Rose* being the latest. Currently Krishna Rose is penning and illustrating her first novel, *Magdalene Speaks—Messiah II*, which she hopes will bring together people of various faiths.

Krishna Vidya Mitchell is a disciple of Gopal Krishna Goswami. She attends and does weekly service at the ISKCON Detroit Devasadhan Mandir. She is a freelance writer and also helps with ISKCON Prison Ministry writing inmates about Krishna Consciousness. Krishna Vidya studied English Literature at Henry Ford Community College and University of Michigan, Dearborn. She intends to engage herself in devotional service in any way she can to spread the Holy Names of Krishna and the culture of Bhakti yoga.

Krsnaa Mary Devi Dasi Fitch is a second generation Hare Krishna, daughter of Akhilananda Das and Mrgaksi Dasi, disciples of Srila Prabhuapda. Growing up away from the temple, she learned how to love the Lord in her heart, through song and storytelling. Living life as a woman and a devotee in modern society has proved to be a challenge. But struggle brings creativity, and Krsnaa's poetry is her way of making sense of it, expressing the pain and the ecstasy of her spiritual evolution. Krsnaa has followed her dreams of acting and writing and graduated from the American Musical & Dramatic Academy in NYC. She has acted in and directed many plays, and is now branching out into film. Her hope is to create a performance art curriculum and philosophy for the modern international devotee community. She feels very fortunate to be included in this poetic anthology, and thanks Krsna Kanta Dasi so much for this wonderful encouragement!

Krsnanandini Devi Dasi is a practitioner of the science of Bhakti yoga under the supervision of his Divine Grace A.C Bhaktivedanta Swami Prabhupada. Her mission is to touch lives and hearts and empower everyone with whom she comes in contact. She serves as a senior minister, mother, wife, and co-director of the Dasi Ziyad Family Institute, as well as president of the Grihastha Vision Team. Krsnanandini is author of several books, curricula and magazine articles including: *Heart and Soul Connection: A Devotional Guide to Marriage, Service, and Love*. For more information visit her website krsnanandini.com.

Krishna-mayi Dasi (Cari Shapiro) met her holy master and eternal guardian, Srila Bhaktivedanta Narayana Maharaja, in May of 2000. Upon that first meeting, he dispelled all of her doubts about life's ultimate goal and the means to achieve it. She saw in him how perfect love could be personified in this world. She would always offer him a poem every time she could attend any of his worldwide festivals. She teaches elementary school, using her experiences with Srila Gurudeva to attempt to serve children with that same type of love as the goal.

Kruti Patel graduated with her Ph.D. in Clinical Psychology and is working as a psychologist in Austin, TX. Her passion lies in blending mental health care with spiritual wellness. She hopes to help devotees deepen their spiritual life through improving their mental health. Spiritual writing and poetry help Kruti stay inspired and connect with Krishna.

Laura Smith: I am currently a student at the University of Virginia studying Sanskrit. My favorite ways to spend my time are cooking for loved ones and experimenting with yummy vegan treats, hosting kirtans for friends, students, and the yoga community in Charlottesville, and going on adventures with my life partner. I've been pursuing devotional life for almost four years, and I cherish discovering and sharing sweet moments of spiritual connection every day.

Madhava Lata Devi Dasi (Marina Matiolli): I was supposed to be born in Brazil, but I was born in Italy; I was supposed to be "another" boy, but I was a girl; I was supposed to graduate as a philosopher, but I ended up working in the IT department of an airlines; I was supposed to brake the social schemes and be an atheist, but I left on a spiritual quest heading to India; I was supposed to work until retirement to get a pension, but instead I choose to run a small hotel ocean-front in the very south of India; when I realized that I wanted to live to the expectations of my heart, I found out that I was a poet.

Madhavi Glick: One experience above all has tremendously blessed my life, April 1999 when I met my spiritual teacher Srila Bhaktivedanta Narayana Goswami Maharaja, a friend and siksha disciple of Srila Prabhupada. After meeting him, I became deeply immersed in Bhakti Yoga. His teachings have provided courage and inspiration to me.

Malvika Unnithan (Madhuri Devi Dasi): Coming from Malaysia to little Durham (UK) was a life changing experience. The heart changing experience came when the Bhakti tradition was shared with me. Love, life, relationships: all these mean so much more to me now. I feel fortunate to be a part of such a loving network of connections.

Mahalaksmi Devi Dasi first encountered Srila Prabhupada's *Bhagavad-gita As It Is* in 1979. Feeling very drawn to the photo of the author on the cover, she recalls how the owner of the book gave it to her saying: "this books seems to be for you." Two years later, Mahakaksmi met Srila Prabhupada's disciples in Majorca, a small Spanish island,

and joined their Sankirtan travelling group, dedicated to distributing his books. After years of such travel she settled in a farm community, married, had three sons and engaged in a variety of services from cow-care to altar service. At present, Mahalaksmi lives in the sacred town of Māyāpur, India. She now devotes herself to producing "audio-books" of Srila Prabhupada's works for Spanish speakers.

Maira J. De La Cruz: I was born in the U.S. in California. I am a lover of music, art, and literature. I follow the path of Bhakti. Having been inspired by visiting the Holy land of India, I am now pursuing a new found dream of sharing my art and poetry in hopes of sparking an awakening in others of their true consciousness. Most of my work is a compilation of personal experiences and inner realizations throughout my spiritual journey of self-discovery. I see my writing as an offering to the Lord and in this way I wish to please him, his devotees, and anyone who happens to read them.

Madhavi Lata Dasi (Maria Shaheen) is both a student and teacher of Bhakti yoga. She has been practicing Bhakti yoga for 24 years, and is a natural teacher. Currently she is assisting with a biography project, being written for her guru, Tamal Krishna Goswami. She lives in Los Angeles, CA.

Mallika Dasi Somershein: The Puru Dynasty of NYC Continues! At age eight, Mallika received initiation from Srila Bhaktivedanta Narayana Maharaja, her beloved inspiration in moving forward on the winding path to true self-discovery and loving action. She currently lives in Honolulu, Hawaii, practicing and studying philosophy, yoga, self-development, numerology, and massage/healing. Watch out! If there is a pen, paintbrush, or paper around, she will pick it up and create something! She hopes to always keep her faith and playful spirit alive through life's lessons, create beauty in the world, and inspire others on their spiritual path.

Malini Jurelius: I was born in Sweden but moved around Europe during my childhood. I went to a performing arts school in Sweden and later switched to composing and writing songs. I love music, dance, and theatre. I travel with Ratha Yatra festivals and perform devotional songs and dances. I believe that music and dance are a joyous way to spread

Krishna consciousness around the world. I love to be part of as much *harinama sankirtana* as I can because I truly believe that is the process that will change everything.

Mandali Dasi, born in 1976, is an internationally acclaimed multidimensional artist. The poems in this volume were written in the early 2000s when Mandali started exploring the artistic abundance and devotional interactions found in the Bhakti practice of worshiping Sri Sri Radha-Krishna deities.

Mandie Howard is a woman who runs with wolves, a mother, student, guide, poetess, explorer, and scientist currently living in Alachua, Florida with her daughter. Through life's many ups and downs, she aspires to row her boat gently and merrily and be, living positively within to share positively without.

Mohini Madhavi Devi Dasi (Maral Alymova Vijay) has a bachelor's degree in computer science and a master's in communication and journalism from the University of Mysore. In her teen years, she won the title of National Chess Champion in the women's division. Today Maral enjoys making Youtube videos, Indian classical dance, karnatik vocals, asthtanga yoga, writing articles and poems. Together with her husband, she runs a small Vedic club called "Blagost" for Russian speaking people in the Bay Area, teaching vedic lifestyle including vegetarian cooking. Her spiritual father is Radhanatha Swami and she lives in Mountain View California with her husband.

Meenakshi is Co-owner/Co-director of Downward Dog Yoga Center and first traveled to India in 1988 to study meditation and philosophy of the Vedas with Swami Shyam in the Himalayas. She is a Certified meditation and Yoga Philosophy teacher from the International Meditation Institute in Kullu, Himalchal Pradesh and has been an international teacher training teacher since 1999 in philosophy, Sanskrit, chanting, meditation, mysore, asthtanga, vinyasa and restorative yoga. Meenakshi is also a practicing Shiatsu Therapist and member of the kirtan band SWAHA.

Mitravinda Devi Dasi: I came to ISKCON in 1981 and have been serving on traveling *sankirtan* distributing Srila Prabhupada's books. From 1983-85 I also served the "Free the Soviet Hare Krishnas" campaign as an undercover agent for ISKCON taking several missions to Moscow. I organized high school preaching and shows for Radio Krishna for ten years as well as produced a smaller version of the back to Godhead magazine in Swedish.

Namita Purohit (Navakishori Devi Dasi) is a trainer, counselor and the founder of Bhakti Women and Build Worthy organizations. She is passionate about investing in human development through her work as a trainer, a coach and a thought partner for people in all seasons and walks of life. She believes in the 360-degree development of people to enable them in becoming high impact change agents for their own selves and society. She provides a rare combination of critical thinking and emotional intelligence.

Nanda (Nancy) Carlson is an evolving poet, writing mostly as reflection, contemplation. Recently, as a student of Bhakti yoga, her poetry has become an expression of her devotion. Nanda works as an Ayurvedic Health Counselor, RN Integrative Health, Wellness and Life Coach, yoga/meditation teacher and Reiki Master. She studies under Satyanarayana Dasa (Babaji) at Jiva Vrindavan and lives in the Boston area. You may contact her on Facebook: Nancy.Carlson.12, or via her website Joyfulhealing.net

Narayani Devi Dasi, a music student of Northwestern University, joined ISKCON in Boston in 1970. She has done many services for Srila Prabhupada including deity worship in Calcutta temple, traveling book distribution in western India for the Bombay temple, and teaching Bhakti Shastri, Bhakti Vaibhava and Bhaktivedanta courses for the VIHE in Vrindavan, India. Narayani helped write the VTE curriculum for Bhakti Shastri and authored s series of 14 books called *Srimad Bhagavat At a Glance*, and *Bhagavad-gita at a Glance*, which features pictures for each of the verses in those texts.

Nirvani Teasley is an aspiring poet/writer, who draws her inspiration from the beautiful island life she shares with her husband of 28 years. When she isn't writing poetry, she is studying the science of evolutionary astrology, her other great passion. Otherwise, you will see her enjoying daily walks in nature and running around with her beautiful grandchildren; and rarely will you see her without a book in hand.

Niscala Dasi

Omika Mali is a recent graduate of Public Health and Psychology from Rutgers University. She is not only interested in creating awareness and empowerment for women voices in ISKCON, but also wants to work in women's health agencies to create effective programs to meet health disparities for women. She aspires to be a life coach for women one day, teaching women to cultivate self worth and motivating them to pursue their callings with determination. In her free time, she enjoys writing about spirituality, mental health and internal change, and loves taking photos and sharing them with messages from the *Bhagavad Gita*.

Paraschiva Florescu is a law student and the founder of the Krishna Consciousness Society in her university. She enjoys writing, studying Vedic scriptures and she has been a classically trained pianist from an early age. Paraschiva chose to focus on developing her connection with God through kirtan. More of her poems can be read at paraskevi96.blogspot.com.

Pooja Singh is an aspiring servant of the devotees, having been introduced to Krishna Consciousness in 2012. She lives in the Washington, D.C. area with her husband and two kids.

Dr. Prachi Desai: I am from Ahmedabad, India. I came into Krishna Consciousness during my college years while studying dentistry in Pune. By birth, I am from a Pushtimarg Vaishnav family. So since childhood I watched my grandmother serve Sri Krishna. When I read Srila Prabhpada's books, I got answers to all the questions I ever had. Although I have been writing poetry since my childhood, nothing fulfills my heart as much as writing poems about Krishna. I work as a dental surgeon in a corporate hospital and have been married for the last two years. I feel privileged that my poem appears in this project. I aspire to be initiated by His Holiness Radhanatha Swami someday and desire to always be of service to the devotees.

Pranada Comtois: Following her guru, Srila A. C. Bhaktivedanta Swami, Pranada Comtois is an exponent of the spiritual evolution of Bhakti's pure love in our lives, our heart, and our relationships. Her writings grow from the joint wisdom of living for twenty years as a contemplative-ascetic in an ashram, then twenty years managing two multi-million dollar businesses, which exemplified practical spirituality in the world. She is a featured speaker in the film *Women of Bhakti*. Deeply affected when witnessing the de-humanizing of women, she was the first to speak up for gender harmony in the modern Bhakti tradition. Pranada successfully organized global steps against gender injustice and published a quarterly journal advocating women's rights. Her passion to inspire and empower women continues to propel her into sacred activism. She can be found at www.pranadacomtois.com. Her forthcoming books *Wise-Love: Bhakti and the Search for the Soul of Consciousness* and *A Swan's Dive: A 50-year Odyssey from Fear into Love* are expected out in September 2017. Her book of poems *Whispers into Twilight* will be released in December 2017.

Priyanka: I came to Newcastle, U.K in 2012 for academic pursuits; little did I know that there was more in store for me than biomedical sciences! In my first month there, I met Radhe Shyama (Roti) and Madhuri (Malvika) who are now two of my closest and dearest friends and who introduced me to Krishna Consciousness. Over the years, as our friendship evolved, so did our journey to Krishna Bhakti. Just when I started feeling a bit lost on my path, thanks to Garuda Prabhu (Graham M. Schweig) I found new light and direction. I have been learning so much about bhakti and the nature of love from all my deep relationships of the heart. I am truly grateful for all the sweet connections.

Promila Chitkara: My name "Promila" is a twisted form of Premila. My name means "full of love." My name holds the purpose of my life—Krishna prem. I'm a technical writer by profession and a creative writer by passion. Krishna orchestrated many synchronicities to bring me to Krishna Consciousness. However, two things that sped up my entry into bhakti were the constant appearance of verse 18.66 of the Bhagavad Gita (my story appeared in BTG: "How Krishna Called Me Back") and *The Journey Home* book by Radhanath Swami.

Radha Cornia is a lawyer, wife, mother, and occasional poet who has been practicing Bhakti yoga for thirty years. She is a graduate of Harvard Law School and is passionate about the protection of women and children. She lives in San Diego where she and her husband run programs aimed at cultivating a community of practitioners of Bhakti yoga.

Radha Mulder was born to an American mother and a Dutch father in Amsterdam, the Netherlands, where she primarily lived for the first 8 years of her life, and thereafter was primarily raised in the state of Hawai'i, in the USA. She was raised in the Vaisnava tradition as her parents were initiated by AC Bhaktivedanta Swami in the early 70's. Radha began writing poetry in her early teens and accredits her inherent strength of spirit and abiding faith, to seeking the deeper meaning of life and bringing its truths to the surface thru the expressive and explorative form of writing poetry. She currently lives in the beautiful and romantic city of Amsterdam, in the Netherlands with her young daughter and is very creative by nature, writing poetry, designing jewelry and clothing and doing photography. www.radhamulder.com

Radha Sundari Devi Dasi (Victoria Ann Taylor): Born in New Zealand, at seventeen Victoria travelled to the US on a Rotary Exchange scholarship. Winning a modeling contest for Seventeen Magazine, she then became a Ford Model and international cover girl. In 1980, she joined ISKCON, took initiation, and was given the name Radha Sundari. In 1984, she married fellow devotee and New Zealand businessman Alister Taylor, (Advaita Chandra), and they moved to Southern California where they raised two children. In 2006, they transferred to Mayapur and together with their family have remained there ever since. Radha Sundari is currently working on a book dealing with life challenges encountered along the path of Bhakti and her journey towards sacred surrender in service of the Divine Mother, Sri Radha.

Raga Swan (Raga Devi Dasi) is a writer, lyricist, and vocalist. She obtained a B.A. in English Lit from Queens College in NYC and has been writing poetry and fiction ever since. Raga published her first poetry book, *Under the Spell of God: Poems for the Lord's Pleasure* in 1995 with Torchlight Publishing. Aiming to attract a wide audience by alluding to a famed theatrical work, she sub-titled her work *Radical Rhymes for Folks Who've Considered Atheism When the Rain-bow was Made By God.*

Rambhoru Devi Dasi (ACBSP) was initiated by Srila Prabhupada in 1974 in Germany and assisted her husband, Prithu Das, establish Krishna Conscious communities in Germany, Iceland, and India. Upon returning to the United States, Rambhoru earned masters degrees in the area of Divinity, Theology, Spiritual Care and Counseling. Rambhoru is currently the Director of the St. Camillus Center for Spiritual Care: Urban Interfaith Chaplaincy program where she educates and supervises professional chaplains in downtown East Los Angeles, CA.

Rukmini Walker (Rukmini Devi Dasi) is the founder of the Urban Devi women's collective. She is an activist in women's spiritual empowerment and interfaith dialogue. She leads workshops and retreats in New York and Washington, D.C. She met her guru, Bhaktivedanta Swami Prabhupada at the age of sixteen and began her lifelong study in Bhakti yoga. She lives in the Washington D.C area with her husband. The kirtan artist Gaura Vani is her son.

Samapriya Devi Dasi (ACBSP) surrendered to Srila Prabhupada in1972. A dedicated book distributor for fifteen years, she spent ten of these in Los Angeles distributing Srila Prabhuapda's books at LAX. During that time she was the main *pujari* (priest) dressing Sri Sri Rukmini Dvarkadesh, the presiding deities of New Dvarka. In 1985 Samapriya and her husband, Dhruva Maharaja, moved to Mayapur, Vrindavan and Jagannatha Puri, living between these three holy dhamas (places) for 28 years. Together they conduct online courses, teaching Srila Prabhupada's books. Samapriya is now compiling her book: an anthology of realizations and poetry entitled *Meditations of a Prabhupada Disciple*.

Seva-mayi Dasi, along with her husband and two school-aged children, resides in New England. She was introduced to Bhakti yoga several years ago and was in a profound state of gratitude when, in the May of 2016, she received the mercy of the shelter of her Guru, and was initiated. She enjoys connecting with nature and oftentimes finds herself writing in the midst of it alongside a river or underneath a grove of trees. Elements found within her philosophy as well as in her everyday *sadhana*, or spiritual practice, oftentimes reveal themselves in the themes and verses of her poetry as she attempts to capture the essence of her experience. Seva-mayi dasi's main passions in life are to serve others—those within her spiritual community as well as all living entities and therefore actively performs community service with her children. She also has an earnest desire for truth and to always seek ways in which to experience deeper levels of devotion and draw closer to Sri Krsna.

Shyama Bhakti Devi Dasi, My first contact with Krishna was during my teenage years, thanks to an American musical group of devotees called *Shelter*. I spent my ashram years serving at a Govinda's Restaurant. Now I find my balance carrying on my spiritual life from home and organizing kirtan events in cultural centers, yoga schools, and wellness fairs. As teaching comes naturally to me, I also organize music classes. Writing is the other activity that immediately connects me to the deeper part of me and to my Lord of the Gopis.

Shyamasundari Dasi lives with her husband and daughter in Alachua Florida. She enjoys visiting the local temple and the string Vaishnava relationships to be found in the community. Her hobbies include writing (she blogs about her journey with her daughter who has special needs) and photography.

Sri Sundari Dasi (Surbhi Kumari): I am a disciple of Indrayumna Swami. I am a practitioner and fan of Bhakti yoga. Academically trained to be a scientist, I have a habit of questioning before believing, and I am grateful to Krishna consciousness for the answers that I continue to receive. While my hobbies include sewing, music, cooking, and painting, my favorite place is in *seva*, or service. My poems reflect my teachers' and Krishna's grace upon me, and I hope that they bring you as much joy as they bring me.

Subhadra was born and raised in a Bhakti yoga community and lives in a rural surrounding in Sweden where she loves to immerse herself in poetry, devotional music, yoga, collecting herbs and gardening. She finds her inspiration from daily reflections, nature, journey, prayer, and relationships... and uses the language of poetry as a way to connect deeper with her heart.

Sudevi Geary is an aspiring writer, pilgrim, and artist; a liminal being, precariously balanced between the archetypal world and the lessons of lived experience. Compulsively nomadic, she carries with her degrees in Social Anthropology, in English with Creative Writing, and the life-long guidance of her guru, Srila Bhaktivedanta Narayana Gosvami Maharaja. Sudevi's writing aims at threading together cross-cultural, spiritual and psychological symbolism to explore the depths of human existence and the soul-journey. She's currently a witness to the spiritual growth of US inmates; assisting in the production of an upcoming art book, and brewing her own literary creations.

Sumati Govinda was born with an intense desire to realize her true nature; a desire that was nurtured by growing up in Satchidananda Ashram-Yogaville. Before she entered kindergarten, her passion for meditation and the Yoga Sutras of Patanjali was ignited. Sumati, her beloved husband, children, and grandchildren call Yogaville home.

Swati Prabhu K.

Taylor F. Bailey lives in Los Angeles, CA, and is a certified massage therapist, actress, and lover of all arts. She is also a practitioner of Bhakti yoga and dedicates the poem she contributed to this book to His Divine Grace Srila Prabhupada.

Theresa Dolan (Tulasi Kunja Devi Dasi): A City Girl in love with Wild Wisdom, Tulasi Kunja looks towards nature to inform us of our own, and uses this as a pathway to study the message of her teachers—that Love is the nature of the Divine. Tulasi has a background in Biological Anthropology and Ecology Curriculum Design, is trained as a Bhakti yoga Instructor, a certified Holistic Nutritionist, and a teacher of Arts and Sciences. She has immense gratitude for her teacher, Radhanath Swami, who paves a framework emblematic of those very personalized ways we experience and hope to embody what is laced with that flash of the heart and transformational nature of the divine: DEVOTIONAL LOVE.

Tivra-bhakti Devi Dasi (Tina Sarayev): I am a mother of three, and in the middle of it all a jewelry artist and a writer (although they are more hobbies than my job). I came in contact with Krishna Consciousness in 2004, moved to an ashram and traveled. It still seems that I have not stopped traveling since, but our family is now somewhat settled in Russel, Canada, where we are a part of the Bhakta Prahlad Primary School: a Montessori style devotee school in its early years.

Tulasi D. Estrella: The words that so melodiously flowed through me one day were never mine but rather yours. Dedicated to Mother Kamagiri Devi Dasi.

Urmila Devi Dasi (Dr. Edith Best) has a Master in School Administration, and a Ph.D. in Educational Leadership, both from the University of Northern Canada at Chapel Hill. She also has master practitioner certification in Neurolinguistic programming. Urmila is a professor of sociology and education at Bhaktivedanta College in Belgium, is acting chair of the shastric (scriptural) Advisory Counsel to ISKCON's Governing Body Commission, and has been an associate editor of Back to Godhead magazine since 1990. She has published *Vaikuntha Children*, a guidebook for devotional education, *The Great Mantra for Mystic Meditation, Sri Manah Siksa*, dozens of articles, and Dr. Best Learn to Read: an 83-book complete literacy program with technology enabling the storybooks to speak in 25 languages at the touch of a special "pen". Urmila has three decades of experience teaching primary and secondary students, which include 19 years as a school administrator and leader.

Vesna Vrindavanesvari is author of the novel *Colored footprints: Live my India* and poetry book: *Never Again Alone*. As a musician, she makes music videos and films featuring lyrics about her spiritual journey creatively incorporating diverse cultural and philosophical elements from her worldwide travels into her artistic expressions. Art is Vesna's way of connecting to a higher nature and God while in this world. She hopes to inspire others to expand and blossom into new inner worlds, new selves and relationships with the eternal Self via her unique creations.

Vicitri Dasi: By the grace of Chaitanya Mahaprabhu, I started coming to India in 1984. Nine years later our Guru-parampara (disciplic succession) brought me to Vrindavan, India to live forever and placed me at the feet of my master, Sri Srimad Bhaktivedanta Narayan Goswami Maharja Finally, after millions of births, someone was capable of caring on a deeply personal level, encountering true, non-sectarian spirit beyond the body: face-to-face with the truth at last! I could never have imagined the joy I experienced traveling with my master. Soon, we will surely reach our goal.

Vidya Devi Dasi (Mary Louise Valerio) is a disciple of Srila Prabhupada, resided in Vrindavan between 1977 and 2001. Her devotional service included caring for Srimati Tulsi Devi and designing deity outfits for temples throughout the world. Vidya is a Vedic astrologer, Ayurvedic healer, and a cook. She teaches and shares these arts with others.

Visakha Dasi (Jean Griesser) received an Associate of Applied Science degree with honors from Rochester Institute of Technology and shortly afterwards published her first book, *Photomacrography: Art and Techniques*. She is the author of five other books, including the memoir "Five Years, Eleven Months and a Lifetime of Unexpected Love," which was a finalist in the Next Generation India Book Awards. She also assists her husband in making documentary films, most recently "Hare Krishna! The Mantra, the Movement, and the Swami who started it all," a 90-minute documentary on the life of Bhaktivedanta Swami Prabhupada, whom she photographed throughout his travels across India, Europe, and the United States. Her website is: our-spiritual-journey.com

Vrinda Sheth is an award-winning author, dancer, and singer. She grew up in Sweden and was raised on stories from the ancient Indian lore, such as the Mahabharata, Ramayana, and Bhagavat Purana. Vrinda lived in Chennai, South India for five years learning classical dance at Kalakshetra, the most reputed institute for Bharata Natyam. It was there that she began to write, and her work has garnered favorable recognition from Kirkus Reviews and won several awards, including the Benjamin Franklin award. She has a B.A. in English from the University of Florida. She now lives in Florida with her husband, daughter, and extended family. To learn more, visit: www.SitasFire.com

Vrindavanesvari Aguilera is a second-generation practitioner of Bhakti yoga, writer, and poet. She has been joyfully engaged for many years as a Montessori early learning teacher-guide at the Bhaktivedanta Academy in Alachua, FL. She is inspired by the wonder and beauty of nature, engaging in and supporting others in all kinds of creative expression, growth, and healing.

Vrindavani Dasi was raised in New Govardhana dham, California; New Raman Reti dham, Florida; and Sri Mayapur dham, India, where she now resides. Creative writing has always been prominent in her life, and she feels that poetry is especially important to Vaishnavas as it is one of the most ideal forms of glorifying the Lord and His devotees.

Vrnda Devi Dasi lives in a hundred-year-old house in Wolseley, the 'granola belt' of Winnipeg, Manitoba, Canada, where she hosts weekly kirtans. Her most recent writing project was a detective novel for pre-teens, *The RAM Club and the Ratha Yatra Rubies*, available on Amazon. Prior to that, she was privileged to edit and contribute to the parenting chapter of the North American Grihastha Vision Team's lovely handbook *Heart & Soul Connection: A Devotional Guide to Marriage, Service and Love*, also available on Amazon.

Vrnda Priya Devi Dasi, whose legal name Darsie Malynn, is a disciple of HH Giriraj Swami. She joined ISKCON in 2009 in Dallas, TX and now resides there. Her desire is to learn how to love Krsna and the devotees, and would like to dedicate these poems to those who have helped her towards this goal.

Yasomati Devi Dasi is originally from Romania and has been practicing Bhakti Yoga for 15 years. She is a disciple of His Holiness Kadamba Kanana Swami. Yasomati has loved writing ever since her childhood when she recalls composing bedtime stories. Later, she began writing poetry and got her first job as a journalist. Unsure if it was proper for devotees to write poetry, she stopped, until a senior Bhakti *yogini* reassured her that one of the qualities of a devotee is to be a poet. Ever since then, her poetry has flowed freely again. She now lives in Sweden.

Zoë Williams: I live in Houston, Texas and I began hearing and learning of Krishna about 4 years ago, through my life partner. This life can seem to bring so much turmoil, it is the moments when I feel still, and listening—opening myself to the words Krishna and devotees have spoken in love—that I can feel my heart at ease, and feel my faith grow. I will continue to chant for, and hear of, and sing to, and dance with, and think of Krishna more and more! Hare Krishna!

GLOSSARY

Achyuta: "The Infallible One," a name for Krishna.

Arjuna: The prince warrior in the *Bhagavad Gita* and close friend of Krishna.

Bhagavad Gita: "The Song of the Divine," the third most read scripture in the world after the Bible and the *Koran*. The most famous text presenting the ethics, philosophy, and theology of Bhakti.

Bhagavata Purana: One of the most beloved scriptural texts of India and Hindu traditions, especially known for its presentation of Krishna's divine acts, both cosmically and intimately.

Bhagavatam: Same as *Bhagavata Purana*, see above.

Bhakta: "One who is absorbed in Bhakti, or devotional love."

Bhakta-vatsala: One who is very beloved to the Bhaktas, or devotees of Krishna.

Bhakti-lata: "The creeper, or vine, of devotional love," referring to the way in which Bhakti grows and thrives.

Bhaktiprappan: An honorific title given to a Bhakti master meaning "one who possesses the greatest humility in Bhakti"

Bhaktisiddhanta: An honorific title given to a Bhakti master meaning "one who possesses the ultimate perfection of Bhakti"

Bhaktivinoda: An honorific title given to a Bhakti master meaning "one who possesses the greatest joy in Bhakti"

Bhaktivedanta: An honorific title given to a Bhakti master meaning "one who possesses the ultimate knowledge in Bhakti"

Bhauma-lila: Divine acts displayed here on this Earthly plane.

Brahmin: A member of the priestly or educating class of traditional Indian society; a Bhakta who is from that class.

Bimba: A reddish colored fruit produced by the ivy gourd tropical vine used to describe the color of Krishna's lips and cheeks. The fruit turns bright red when ripe.

Chaitanya: (1486-1533) The medieval mystic love saint who founded Vaishnavism in Bengal and spread it to northern and southern India, popularizing the congregational chanting of the Mahamantra, revered by his followers as a divine descent and embodiment of the love shared between Radha and Krishna.

Chamara: A Himalayan yak-tail fan used in worship ceremonies in Hindu temples.

Chintamani: A magical gemstone that exists in the spiritual realm of Divinity through to have certain auspicious powers, and the ability to fulfill the wishes of one who possesses it.

Darshan: "Seeing the Divine," or having an audience with a sacred image or person.

Devaki-Nandan: "The joy of Devaki (Krishna's mother)," a name for Krishna.

Dholak: A popular percussion instrument used in dancing *kirtans* as it can be strung around the neck and played while standing.

Diksha: An initiation ritual involving a guru formally accepting a disciple in Hindu traditions.

Gajendra: "The Greatest of Elephants," a personality in the sixth book of the *Bhagavat Purana*, who becomes wholly dependent on Krishna's grace.

Ganga: Same as the River Ganges; one of the most sacred rivers in India.

Gaura: "The Golden One," a name for Chaitanya.

Goloka: The divine world of Krishna and his beloveds.

Gopal: "The loving protector of cows," a name for Krishna.

Gopi: "A cowherd maiden or woman," a member of the group of Gopis, Krishna's greatest beloveds.

Gopinath: "The beloved Lord of the Gopis," a name for Krishna.

Goswamis: An honorific title for a *sanyassin* or a celibate monk.

Govardhan: The special hill or mountain that Krishna lifts to protect the residents of the divine realm of Vraja from Indra's wrath.

Govinda: "The one who herds the cows," a name for Krishna.

Gunas: The essential "qualities" arising from primordial nature that constitute this world and to which the residents of this world are subject.

Hari: "The one who steals our hearts," a name for Krishna.

Hari bol: "Chant the name of Hari or Krishna"

Hari-katha: Sharing or conversing about Krishna and his divine acts.

Hiranyakashipu: The ruthless tyrannical king and father or saintly Sri Prahlad, who was killed by the great and powerful manifestation of Krishna as Narasimhadeva.

Ishvari: Referring to the divine Goddess in a cosmic sense.

ISKCON: "The International Society for Krishna Consciousness," the Hare Krishna Movement that A.C Bhaktivedanta Swami founded in 1966.

Jaladutta: The mercantile ship on which Prabhupada sailed over oceans from India to America, that docked in Boston harbor when he first arrived.

Japa: The soft and gentle recitation of sacred mantras in meditation.

Jiva: The individual, life-giving self within each sentient being.

Kaliya: The multi-headed, poisonous serpent on whose heads Krishna danced while conquering him.

Kartalas: Small brass hand-cymbals traditionally played in rhythm in outdoor *kirtans*, or congregational chanting parties.

Kartika: The lunar month in autumn at the height of the harvest season, believed to be the holiest month of the year and the season during which the great rasa dance of Krishna took place.

Kavacha: "Shield," or protective holy relic or amulet.

Kinkoris: Young girls under the age of e

Kirtana: Congregational or group chanting in which a single singer leads a call and response chant often accompanied by musical instruments.

Kumkuma: Red vermillion powder used to decorate married women in India on various parts of their body, particularly the part of their hair and feet.

Kunja: "Forest grove," usually referring to the secret meeting places in the woods of Vrindavan where Krishna would meet his beloved Gopis.

Madana-mohan: "The one who bewilders Cupid, or the god of love with his beauty," a name for Krishna.

Madhava: "The Sweetest Lord," a name for Krishna.

Madhu: Honey

Mahamantra: "The most powerful mantra for deliverance and liberation in this age," Hare Krishna Hare Krisna Krishna Krishna Hare Hare, Hare Rama Hare Rama Rama Rama Hare Hare, popularized originally by Chaitanya in the 16th century.

Mahamaya: "The powerful force of illusion," one of Krishna's principle, eternal energies.

Mangala arati: The specific early morning, first-of-the-day service held before the sacred images of Radha and Krishna.

Maya: The illusive energy of Krishna either reinforcing the conditioning of souls in bondage to this world or reinforcing the loving relationships in the divine world.

Mayapura: One of the primary pilgrimage sites for practitioners of the Chaitanya school of Bhakti; a town in west Bengal resting between the rivers Ganges and Sarasvati, believed to be where Chaitanya first appeared over 500 years ago.

Mogra: A species of jasmine flower native to a small region in the Eastern Himalayas in Bhutan, India, and Pakistan, which is referred to in ancient Vedic texts as a favored decoration for the Gopis and Krishna.

Mridanga: A percussion double-headed drum typically made of clay and bound together by cowhide, designed to be portable to be played in "walking *kirtans*", or *padayatras*.

Nama: "Name," usually referring to the divine names.

Nama sankirtana: Congregational chanting of the holy names of Krishna and his consort, Radha.

Nandulal: "The darling of Nanda"; A name for Krishna indicating how dear he was to his father, Nanda.

Nandana: "Experiencing joy"

Narashimhadeva: The half-man, half-lion form of Krishna who vanquished the tyrannical king Hyranyakashipu, and offers protection to his devotees.

Nityananda Balarama: The name of Lord Chaitanya's brother (Nityananda) which indicates that he is a divine descent of Krishna's brother, Balarama.

Nityananda Prabhu: The name of Lord Chaitanya's brother.

Pancha-tattva: The five principles of Divinity manifest as Lord Chaitanya and his four other divine companions.

Pancha-veni: Five braids, as in when rivers meet.

Parampara: Lineage of teachers or initiating gurus in the Bhakti tradition.

Parivara: A specific lineage of teachers.

Pranama: Offering of respects or honoring another, or the divine.

Prabhupada: Honorific title given to especially exalted teachers in the bhakti tradition.

Prema: Purest Love, or Love of God, Divine Love.

Pujari: A priest in Hindu culture that is trained in the rituals of sacred image worship.

Radha: A name for the Supreme Goddess in the bhakti tradition, Radha: the Supreme Divine Feminine counterpart to Krishna's Supreme Divine Masculine.

Radha Damodara: Two of the most prominent names of the Divine Feminine (Radha) and Divine masculine (Damodara).

Radhika: A name for the Supreme Goddess in the bhakti tradition, Radha: the Supreme Divine Feminine counterpart to Krishna's Supreme Divine Masculine.

Rajasthanis: Residents of Rajasthan, in Northern India.

Rati-keli: The amorous divine acts (or *lilas*) of the Supreme Divine Couple in the Bhakti tradition, Radha and Krishna.

Rotis: A fried flat bread popular in Indian cooking.

Satsvarupa: "The essential form of spirit"

Sadhu: A holy man

Samskara: A psychological impression upon one's consciousness that can bear positive or negative effects. In Hindu tradition, typically referring to rituals performed for personal benefit.

Seva: "Service"

Shyama: "The dark one", a name for Krishna.

Shyamasundara: "The beautifully dark one", a name for Krishna.

Sri Chaitanya: (See Chaitanya above).

Sri Yugala: A name given to the Divine Couple Radha and Krishna, particularly referring to one of the ritualistic ceremonies—or *aratis*—in which they are worshiped.

Sridham Navadvipa: The sacred nine ("nava") islands ("dvipas")—or the abode of the nine types of devotional service in the Bhakti tradition—where Lord Chaitanya appeared. Four of the "islands" are situated on the eastern side of the River Ganges in West Bengal, and five are situated on the western side.

Swamini: A female swami, or holy teacher. A name used for Radha, Krishna's consort, who is the ultimate teacher in the Bhakti tradition.

Tilaka: A specific marking painted upon various parts of the body of Hindus, especially the forehead. Vaishnava *tilak* is made with sacred clay consisting of two vertical lines representing Krishna's toe, met at the bottom by a leaf symbol, representing a holy Tulasi leaf.

Tulasi Devi: A sacred goddess in the Bhakti tradition, most dear to Krishna, who is believed to reside in all Holy Basil plants for the benefit of her worshipers. It is from the wood of these plants that the sacred beads upon which Bhakti yogis chant upon are made. All initiated Vaishnavas also wear three strands of Tulasi beads around their necks.

Tulasi Puja: The worship ceremony performed every morning and evening unto the sacred Tulasi plant in Hindu, and especially Vaishnava culture.

Vaijayanti: Name of the beautiful flower garland worn by Krishna.

Vaikuntha: "Free from anxiety", a name given to heavenly realms where there is an absence of any kind of stress, misery or anxiety.

Vaishnava: A worshiper of Vishu, or Krishna.

Viraja River: According to ancient Hindu cosmology, this is the river that serves as a border between the spiritual and physical universes.

Vraja: The divine world of Krishna and his love which is connected to the Vraja region in this world near Agra, India.

Vrindavan: "A forest filled with Vrinda, or sacred Tulasi trees"; the sacred realm of Krishna's divine childhood acts; see Vraja.

Yantra: A two dimensional geometrical symbol and meditational object and visual used for elevating consciousness.

Yashoda: A name for Krishna's mother who raised him in Vrindavan.

Yashomati-Nandan: "The joyful son of Yashoda"; a name for Krishna.

Yogamaya: "The divine power that brings about loving union"; Krishna's divine energy through which he manifests himself; the divine Goddess who makes arrangements within Krishna's dive acts for loving connections with souls.

Yogini: A female practitioner of yoga

Yugala Kishora: The youthful couple of Radha and Krishna.

ACKNOWLEDGEMENTS

This book emerged from the *Kavirani Project*, started fourteen years ago to honor the valuable voices of the women in the Bhakti tradition through publishing their poems. Although I envisioned the project would easily draw in 108 contributors, it wasn't until I engaged social media—only in the last two years—and founded the *Vaishnavi Voices Poetry Project*—that I was able to find enough participants. I am therefore grateful to modern technology for facilitating the search and providing a suitable forum in which the project developed.

Many thanks to those special souls whose enthusiasm for the project, and subsequent efforts, also helped draw in new participants: my inspiring friends David B. Wolf and Marie-Helene Glasheen-Buffin of the Satvatove Institute, Vicitri Dasi whose support was very uplifting to me, the dear Rukmini Walker, whose love and encouragement blew fresh wind into my sails, and especially, Pranada Comtois, whose spiritual activism to empower women has inspired me since I was a teenager. Thank you also to all others who spread the word about the project, including the online journals The Tattooed Buddha, ISKCON News and Rebelle Society.

My heartfelt appreciations to the five dedicated and talented Vaishnavi editors who patiently worked with me over the last three years in carefully organizing and selecting the hundreds of poems that flowed into the project. Madhava Lata Devi Dasi reviewed the submissions for philosophical accuracies, while Seva Mayi Dasi, Jasmine Kang and Subhadra sensitively offered suggestions for thematic and aesthetic sorting. Together, their reliable, spirited involvement carried this project the distance.

I am especially thankful to the last member of the editorial team, my dearest friend Vrindavanesvari Aguilera—a wonderful poet herself—whose ever-attentive care, love, and guidance provided endless encouragement and inspiration throughout the various phases of book production in all kinds of delightful ways.

I extend a warm, grateful hug to each of the nine wonderful women who wrote the diverse chapter introductions: Rukmini Walker (Rukmini Devi Dasi), Vishaka Devi Dasi (Jean Griesser), Pranada Comtois, Urmila Devi Dasi, Arcana Siddhi Devi Dasi, Braja Sorensen, Vrinda Sheth, Dhanya Rico and Janavi Held. The book has been significantly enriched because of them.

Special thanks to Raghu Consbruck of Ragu Designs for the beautiful book cover design she generously volunteered to create for us, and to Lisa Saraswati Devi Cawley for the gorgeous lotus photograph she gifted us to adorn its front.

Much gratitude, as always, to my wonderful publisher *par excellence*, Alice Maldonado Gallardo, of Golden Dragonfly Press, whose professionalism, love of what she does, and beautiful work always makes her a pleasure to collaborate with.

My love to Srimati Syamarani Dasi, and my sisters in the Srila Bhaktivedanta Narayana Goswami sanga, who welcomed me into their fold when my spiritual father left this world on Guru Purnima 2003, and who have no fear or hesitation of blossoming in all the beautiful ways that their beloved Gurudeva wants them to.

This book would have never been possible without the loving grace and inspiration of A.C Bhaktivedanta Swami Prabhupada, whose devoted disciples first introduced me to Bhakti yoga. I owe a special debt to a particular disciple of his, my dearest husband, Garuda Das, who kindly wrote the Foreword, prepared the Sanskrit Glossary and whose loving encouragement always brings out the best in me.

Lastly, with heartfelt obeisance, I thank my own beloved spiritual father, Srila Bhaktiprappan Damodar Goswami, who once told me—over twenty years ago in a little ashram in Puri— that he envisioned me writing books that would inspire others in their practice of Bhakti. May the offering of this book begin to fulfill that generous vision! And may Vaishnavis everywhere feel as supported in sharing their own individual, valuable gifts as I was by him.

Made in United States
Troutdale, OR
12/22/2023